Responsible Dominion

Responsible Dominion

A Christian Approach to Sustainable Development

IAN HORE-LACY

REGENT COLLEGE PUBLISHING
Vancouver, British Columbia

Published 2006 by Regent College Publishing
5800 University Boulevard, Vancouver, BC V6T 2E4 Canada
Web: www.regentpublishing.com
E-mail: info@regentpublishing.com

Views expressed in works published by Regent College Publishing are those of the author and do not necessarily represent the official position of Regent College <www.regent-college.edu>.

All the royalties from this book have been irrevocably assigned to Langham Literature (formerly the Evangelical Literature Trust), a programme of the Langham Partnership International (LPI) and Langham UK and Ireland. Langham Literature distributes evangelical books to pastors, theological students and seminary libraries in the Majority World, and facilitates the writing and publishing of Christian literature in regional languages. For further information on Langham literature, and the other programmes of LPI, visit the website at <www.langhampartnership.org>.

Unless otherwise noted, Scripture from *The Holy Bible, English Standard Version* copyright © 2001 by Crossway Bibles, a division of Good News Publishers. Used by permission. All rights reserved.

Library and Archives Canada Cataloguing in Publication Data

Responsible dominion : a Christian approach to sustainable development
/ Ian Hore-Lacy

Includes bibliographical references.
ISBN 1-57383-342-8

1. Environmental ethics 2. Nature—Religious aspects—Christianity
3. Sustainable development—Religious aspects—Christianity 4. Human
ecology—Religious aspects—Christianity. I. Title.

BT695.5 H67 2006   261.8'8

Contents

Preface

Since the early 1990s there have been numerous valuable Christian contributions to understanding how people should interact with and view God's creation. However, these have tended to follow the secular response to environmental issues, focusing on the old agenda of environmental integrity considered in isolation from people and their resource needs. They have also been primarily academic in source and perspective, and represent God's purposes in the world as if it were a big national park without the inconvenience of six billion people.[1] None grapple with today's Sustainable Development agenda which, particularly since the 2002 World Conference on Sustainable Development held in Johannesburg, is increasingly focused on poverty eradication and the needs of people generally.

This book sets out to add to this thinking in two respects:

• What is the appropriate human role *vis á vis* God's Creation?— what is sound Christian stewardship of God's abundant provision? and in particular,

• What is practical and sustainable, especially in relation to land use, food production, minerals and energy?

It is axiomatic that these perspectives are not in conflict but are mutually supporting. That is to say, what is 'sustainable', if it is not also practical and a proper expression of Christian stewardship, is not going to take us very far. However, it is in relation to the practical aspect that the book seeks to break some new ground in the Christian context, and balance the valuable contributions of other authors on aspects of stewardship. But as I point out: without some knowledge of the relevant facts and a little understanding of the ideological battleground, Christians can uncritically support positions which are counterproductive to faithful stewardship of God's creation. Some—on careful examination—may even be pagan.

Stewardship here is presented as the wise and active management of what has been abundantly provided for humankind by a loving Creator.

Modern environmentalism, I contend, has often been shown as deficient, with (barely) hidden agendas inimical to human values. While claiming the moral high ground, it is populist, ideologically-driven and ultimately counterproductive of its own declared aims. In contrast, Christian stewardship of God's creation should be a response to an understanding that God has provided very liberally for us. It involves attention to the human economy as well as the natural ecology. Science and technology bring these aspects together and provide the tools for the job.

Christians above all should resist the green agenda which puts six billion people in second place to some narrow, idealised concept of 'the environment'. A major question is: to what extent is today's Christian environmentalism pagan? Christians should understand that they can virtuously apply their lives to meeting people's needs by focusing on the utilitarian aspects of creation without losing sight of the need for care and respect.

It has been fun compiling as a popular and accessible book since it traverses many aspects of my life over the last 40 years, through farming, conservation activism, forest ecology, education, environmental science, mining, nuclear energy and Christian involvement in ideas and issues. I hope that alone makes it more practical and useful to those engaged in the world's practical vocations than other treatments of these matters!

Ian Hore-Lacy

Acknowledgements

Many people have contributed to this book, either deliberately or inadvertently. Foremost have been those whose thoughts and discussion have prompted my own thinking and research over many years. Attempting to name even a representative selection from 35 years involvement in environmental and corporate spheres risks serious omissions, but the inputs have certainly spanned that time.

Some of the material has been developed in the context of discourse within Zadok and ISCAST in Australia and (for chapter 2) the John Ray Initiative in UK, indeed some parts of several chapters have developed through publication by Zadok and ISCAST with subsequent feedback. I gratefully acknowledge the role of such discourse through both meetings and publications in forming my ideas and honing them to the point where I have the confidence to offer them for wider publication.

The fact that most of those with whom I have interacted in Christian fellowship are aligned with academia rather than business, and see or approach the world from a very different standpoint, has both stimulated me and sharpened the output. While esteeming them and valuing their contributions, I do not expect them to greet what I have to say with boundless enthusiasm! But nor do I expect the book to be cheered on by those with a basically utilitarian view of resources and environment, though they too have provided a reality check at times.

The figure in Chapter 4 was developed by me while I was with CRA Limited (now Rio Tinto), and my twenty years in that corporate fold allowed me to develop much of the understanding of minerals, energy and land use which is central to the book. My understanding of how people perceive and champion the environment, and the profound clash of values involved, has been crystallised in discussions when I have been aligned with the nuclear power industry.

En route to publication several people have helpfully contributed to parts of the MS: Professor Sam Berry and Sir John Houghton (chapter 2), Peter Fagg and Jamie (Jack) Allen (ch 3), and Jon Clark. I am particularly grateful to Chris Davey for his detailed review of the manuscript at draft stage, and encouragement to expound the notion of God as Provider more fully.

Introduction

In the beginning God created the Heavens and the Earth.* The Earth with its moon was part of the solar system of planets revolving around the sun, the Earth's orbit defining one year. The sun was the source of much of the world's energy, and was in turn part of a wider galaxy. The Earth was endowed with many minerals as part of its geological structure, which was good. The minerals were able to form soil.

At the outset, some 4500 million years ago, the Earth was formless and devoid of life but was made to rotate on its axis so that sunlight fell on every part of its surface and differentiated day from night in each place, and the rotation defined one day. The Spirit of God was involved in all this creative activity, which God saw was good.

God made the atmosphere separate from the oceans and made the land emerge from the oceans, but allowed for continuing adjustment between land and sea through crustal movements both lateral and vertical as well as geomorphological processes of erosion, deposition and forming further rocks. This too was good.

---

* A paraphrase or integrative interpretation of the creation account in Genesis 1:1-26 in terms of currently-understood cosmology, rather than the original prescientific metaphor.

Then God created life, both plants and animals in the sea and on the land. As this life evolved over more than 2000 million years, it multiplied in diversity and increased in complexity under God's oversight. Some animals learned to fly, while some animals and plants became extinct. Some animals became intelligent and dexterous, which underlined how good was God's creation.

All the plants and animals reproduced with others of their kind so that populations were in continuing dynamic balance with their resources. God made the living things and their ecological balance and processes good.

Then, having bounteously equipped the world with every imaginable resource, in abundance, God said 'let us make humans in our image, in our likeness, and let them rule over the rest of creation'.

This book aims to unpack and expound some of the implications of that last sentence in the context of where we all are early in the 21st century.

The Continuing Story

As we reflect upon human progress and interaction with the world environment up to the end of the 20th century a number of things are evident. We have increased fourfold—from 1.6 to 6.0 billion people over the course of that century, while on average we are each four times better off.[1] This has been enabled by increased food production, the availability of cheap energy—giving a 13-fold increase in energy use, and the ready availability of fresh water to population centres. At the same time we have changed the surface of the planet more than ever before, mainly through agriculture. We have also caused massive pollution in many parts of the world but have responded to this heroically and reversed much of it,[2] though much remains to be done.

Today the resource and environmental challenges are greater than ever before, leading some to cry doom and gloom, even as others dismiss all fears. While it is clear that we cannot continue without changing the way we do many things, there is no reason to believe that the ongoing transition to a more sustainable world economy will not continue. Limits to growth have constantly been extended. Christian insights on stewardship of God's creation have much to contribute in this transition in helping to counter narrow and extreme agendas, and enlightening the secular mindset which tends towards greed and selfish exploitation.

There is a clear stream of Western culture which is detached from any Christian sensitivity or constraints and which has approached the natural world exploitively, carelessly and unconscionably and which has consequently caused much environmental damage and waste of resources. This is perhaps seen most strongly in the former Soviet Union, where technological arrogance was politically unconstrained. Though it obviously frames much of the discussion, this ultimately secular and totally utilitarian approach[3] falls largely outside the scope of this book, which focuses on appropriate Christian responses to resources and environment questions in the context of modern environmental sensitivity and green ideology.

With Friends of the Environment Like These, Who Needs Enemies?

One of the greatest changes in Western society over the past 40 years has been the progression from indifference to the concern for the quality of the environment. That is basically good, and Christians who see the environment as a vital aspect of the world created by God can welcome it. Indeed, most have followed it.

But the new outlook carries some baggage. The change had two related drivers. First was deteriorating air and water quality, land degradation and the encroachment of development on landscapes and ecosystems. These caused public demand for regulation to curb pollution and development. The second driver was environmental groups campaigning through membership and media to raise public awareness. From the nineteenth century these groups tended to represent scientifically (and especially biologically) informed citizens,[4] but in the 1970s ideology became the prime motivator in many of the groups, and this persists. The values involved are discussed later.

The chief effect of the 1970s transition was to drive the policy of environmental groups away from science-based analysis, and into political advocacy and activist campaigns, which sometimes had little to do with environmental quality and nature conservation values. Indeed, some are quite counterproductive to such.

Many of the older people now cast as environmental optimists (or simply beyond the pale) have served their apprenticeship in or around the radical end of the environmental spectrum. To some extent I am one of those. We have joined the chorus of strident protest, urged speedy attention to environmental insults regardless of cost, castigated self-interested and apathetic politicians, and dreamed utopian dreams in solidarity with a community of like-minded people. We were enlightened and our secular (or was it moral and spiritual?) mission was to change the world according to our values.

Some of us took our green values and motivation into professional life, in my case as biology teacher in a high school and then environmental scientist in industry. In that context, when one was actually faced with doing something about pollution and resolving land use questions justly and practically, the world started to look a bit different. The single issue could not be considered on its own, it meshed inexorably with many other issues. The local 'fix' sometimes had wider ramifications. The moral opposition to ecological and climate change intersected with other moral issues more immediately related to people's needs.

This is where the episodic flirting of the green movement with business is fascinating. There is an awareness that whether by coercion or persuasion, the practitioners in every branch of industry must be the ones whose work brings about improved environmental quality. The problem is, those people are alien to the values of the main green pressure groups, so their motives are suspect and disparaged. Furthermore there is active opposition to their actual endeavours due to any of several agendas—from anti-globalisation and anti-capitalism to the values discussed below. The effects of this antipathy are not trivial. The current push for corporate social responsibility as an overarching principle of corporate governance does not address the dilemma. Beyond articulating responsible behaviour, it is arguably more about appeasement of those hostile to corporate enterprise and capitalism than achieving new outcomes—such as could be done by sensible government.

The hidden agendas here have serious implications socially and politically. They mean that activist campaigns in some cases lose sight of human need, and they can drive the political process (via public opinion) in wasteful directions through sustained misinformation. The media[5] is the vehicle, through journalists whose activism or eagerness to produce a gripping story sometimes eclipses their professionalism.

The latest example of ideology displacing science, and through scare campaigns affecting government policy, is in relation to genetic manipulation of plants ('tampering with nature') and genetically-modified (GM) foods in particular. The motivating ideology is veneration of a particular concept of nature,[6] and the methodology is well-orchestrated incitement of fear (Frankenstein Foods, etc). The result is that Europe is largely without the benefits of those foods. Thus far, it is no great problem for consumers, but it is the thin edge of a very large wedge and jeopardises the technology which promises to do much to deliver more food to more of the world's six billion inhabitants. It is addressed in a later chapter.

Another example is regarding ionising radiation. Misusing a conservative principle designed to be applied in radiation protection, the green groups incite fear by proclaiming that 'there is no safe level of radiation', and purport to quote scientific radiation protection bodies in this.[7] Therefore no effort or expense should be spared to minimise radiation exposure, even at trivial levels, and any technology to do with radiation must be opposed as technocratic irresponsibility. This conveniently ignores the fact that we are all exposed to significant levels of natural background radiation at 2-3 units,[8] that some are exposed to much more naturally (ranging up to 100 units and more) without ill effect. It also ignores the fact that there is scant scientific evidence of any harm to anyone at the sort of levels under discussion (less than 50 units). Once again, it is an ideologically-based campaign using fear and ignorance to manipulate public opinion. (There is in fact now mounting evidence that low doses of radiation—below 50 units—may sometimes have beneficial effects.)

Radiation is of course closely related to the anti-nuclear energy campaign, equally fear-laden,[9] and with a set of folklore which is impervious to facts. This has had the effect of causing massive government subsidies to technologies such as wind and solar generation which, whatever their virtues, can never deliver the same as nuclear power—continuous, reliable electricity supply on a large scale, which happens to be what industrial societies require. The issue is discussed further in chapter 5, the point here is the character of opposition brought to bear.

A third example is forest protection campaigns in Australia and North America. Science is spurned in favour of images of mature or 'old growth' forests whose protection is sought by appeal to public sentiment. This then drives management policies administered by urban bureaucrats. Such policies either avoid logging in particular ecologically sound ways or avoid appropriate fire management, either way threatening the long-term viability of the ecosystem. In February 2004 the Australian Broadcasting Corporation made a current affairs program on Tasmanian forestry purporting to show delinquent mismanagement. It won a prestigious award for environmental journalism. In December, following an appeal to the complaints tribunal, the ABC conceded that the program was unfair, biased, inaccurate and emotive, and apologised to Forestry Tasmania and the companies concerned.[10] Forest management can readily be driven by green sentiment devoid of scientific underpinning into policies which achieve exactly the opposite of sustainable environmental and resource management. This question is addressed further in a later chapter.

Christians are quite properly attracted to any endeavours to address environmental concerns. The internationally-respected John Stott has put it clearly[11]: 'We must learn to think and act ecologically. We repent of extravagance, pollution and wanton destruction. We recognise that human beings find it easier to subdue the Earth than to subdue themselves.' But without some knowledge of the relevant facts and a little understanding of the ideological battleground, Christians can uncritically support positions which are counterproductive to faithful stewardship of God's creation.

This book is designed to shed some light into some of those murky areas, and while not always providing answers, at least highlighting the issues in contention.

The perspectives canvassed here are contentious on several fronts. Even among those who acknowledge God as creator and humankind as having some kind of stewardship role, there are many different viewpoints and approaches. This provides both a challenge and opportunity for Christians to transcend entrenched positions by a preoccupation with Truth and a rejection of self interest as primary motivation.

Christian insights on God as Provider for people in the context of his creation take the concept of stewardship of creation rather wider than the green agenda as expounded by many Christian writers during the 1990s. While theirs remains a valid view and emphasis, it should not be represented as a Christian consensus, let alone an enduring one. Nor is it sustainable in the context of meeting human needs. It tends to echo uncritically the green movement's priority of environmental preservation over the needs and aspirations of the developing world. There are some ideological currents in all this which in my view have no defensible theological basis but are readily picked up by Christian environmental apologists[12].

I hope that the following chapters establish that there are some distinctives to a Christian view of stewardship of creation, and while it would be unrealistic to suggest that Christians were thereby divorced from the philosophical and other allegiances discussed in this Introduction, it is important that we can transcend them, at least to some degree. The challenge is similar to that for Christians interacting with politics, not to be totally captive to any particular position, nor unable to see and appreciate issues from other perspectives.

The underlying contention is the fundamental disagreement with those who portray human influence and interests as generally bad, inappropriate environmentally, and inevitably damaging.[13] These usually assert 'the environment' as being more important than people, which is not a position congenial to most Christians. On the other hand the environment does have particular intrinsic value and importance, as outlined in the next chapter.

Values in tension

The application of technology, particularly to genetic manipulation and to energy options as discussed in later chapters, is fraught by a clash of value systems.

The dynamics of the environmental movement as it has matured over the last 30 years suggests that there is a tension between two paradigms, whereby nature and the environment is perceived predominantly as either:

• **a physical construct**, understood and approached scientifically and rationally, and having instrumental or utility values, or

• **a moral construct**, 'nature', understood metaphysically and having aesthetic and spiritual values, which are intrinsic.

There are obviously those who identify primarily with each. The first has a strong basis among those who championed the environment cause in the 1960s, as the side effects of industrialisation became widely recognised and challenged. The second followed it at a popular level, though its roots are as old as human thought, as discussed in chapter 1. Because the second tends to be economically marginalised and radical, it throws up passionate and committed advocates who feel that they have a monopoly on ethics. But most people span both paradigms to some degree. Operationally they accept the first, but with reservations which make them open to the second, and seeking the satisfaction of some alignment with it.[14] A major challenge, addressed in this book, is to avoid dualism and develop a coherent balance between the two so that the developers maintain a sensitivity to the metaphysical and the neo-romantics address the practical issues intelligently.

Another way of looking at the question is in terms of Maslow's hierarchy, with people's basic needs being abundantly met in the Western world, so that their attention turns to the higher level of self-actualisation and all the diverse elements which may be involved, particularly anything related to quality of life. This may be extended to avoidance of risk. It may be assumed here that all of us are motivated in some degree to pursue the common good even if this involves some personal sacrifice and effort beyond narrow self-interest. The problem is that definition of the common good is not always widely shared, and in particular there is divergence in relation to balancing risks and benefits at a community level.

Reservations about the first paradigm readily arise from observing people who operate largely on the basis of it, and whose values are limited to instrumental rather than aesthetic appreciation of nature, or who espouse 'a doctrine of freedom with the ethics squeezed out'.[15] Many such critical observers on the other hand are likely to see the environment as a factor of social critique and perhaps dissent, the latter taking the form of some degree of simplified lifestyle.

This clash of values is highlighted in the proposition that totalitarianism is implicit in technological choices such as nuclear power or other large-scale enterprises which lock citizens powerlessly inside the system needed to sustain those technologies. Therefore we need to restructure society's technological base around human-scale, democratic technologies[16] and steer away from obvious risks (even if we thereby commit to greater but less-obvious ones). This is a commonly expressed sentiment but the conclusion is questionable in a world of six billion inhabitants, more than half of whom justifiably aspire to distinctly improved living standards. Nor is it conceded that citizens feeling oppressed by the scale of technology or cities cannot move to more congenial (and probably economically poorer) surroundings. It relates to another and contrary accusation made in the same discussion[17] that environmentalism is an ideology which is associated with utopian, and where opportunity permits, totalitarian programs for the complete reformation of human life.

Other writers bring insights on how these paradigms are expressed, contrasting two modern streams of environmentalism with roots in the Romantic and Rational traditions. Maurie Cohen sees postmaterialism as the engine of environmentalism in countries such as Sweden and Netherlands, while Japan and Norway stand out as having a more pragmatic conception of nature, with greater reliance on science in understanding nature and technology in their approach to environmental quality.[18]

There is a clear propensity by a large part of the environmental movement to use the concept of the 'environment' as a stalking horse for political agendas without engaging seriously with sustainable development. Avner De-Shalit[19] calls this 'conceptual environmentalism' and suggests that it is a deliberate tactic rather than a straightforward expression of values. For instance he sees Deep Ecology as a political theory based in faulty science and pop psychology, rather than being an expression of environmental ethics, and he quotes advocates of it who refer to its 'metaphysical teachings'. De-Shalit concludes by lamenting the conflation of environmental philosophy and political theory, and suggests it might 'be better for the environment if we concentrate separately on the moral grounds for environmentalism and the democratic theory about the institutions which best guarantee a cleaner environment, animal welfare, etc., let alone social justice.' This would be widely supported among those working on the basis of the first paradigm, and helpfully makes the point that the clash of values is not simply rational utilitarianism versus moral principle.

More starkly, Hugh Mackay, a respected social researcher says (of the Australian political party), 'The Greens represent the new world religion—a modern version of pantheism—whose fundamentalist church is Greenpeace. Their political strength springs from the perception that they are being true to values that, deep down, most of us feel inclined to accept.'[20]

There is no lack of writers who see green extremism as incorrigible and hostile to both democracy and Western civilisation. For instance James Sheehan[21] writing about 'Global Greens' asserts that 'Green zealots are not likely to be moved' by the evident social and economic benefits from international resource development, and he warns that 'no company should underestimate the moral righteousness that motivates so many in the movement'. 'Oil, gas and mineral extraction industries are directly in the crosshairs of NGO[22] activism today'. Alston Chase is similarly clear that North American resource industries are engaged in a battle born of divergent values.[23] Hugh Morgan, when Chief Executive of a major resource company with well-established environment management credentials, ten years ago said[24] that 'contemporary environmentalism, in its pure form, is as radical and uncompromising an attack on the entire structure of Western society as can be imagined.' I have heard this echoed many times since.

Christian stewardship of creation will necessarily feel the tension of the two paradigms, because both express some truth. In the political process within Western democracies, both paradigms need expression. But at the interface of aid and trade with developing countries the picture is sometimes unhappy, with the danger of inappropriate values being foisted on people who do not have social and political mechanisms to decide on what is best for them.

This book aims to explore how Christians, individually and collectively, might approach today's Sustainable Development agenda. This is increasingly focused on poverty and thus brings in the notion of resources as God's provision for people. This book sets out to add to and in some cases counter the Christian environmental writings of the 1990s in two respects:

• What is the appropriate human role vis á vis God's Creation?— what is sound Christian stewardship of God's abundant provision? In particular,

• What is practical and sustainable, especially in relation to land use, food production, minerals and energy?

1

Stewards of God the Provider

Loving God,
we thank you for this world of wonder and delight.
You have given it to us to care for,
so that all your creatures may enjoy its bounty.

This thanksgiving prayer,[1] designed for use when Christians come together in community, summarises the framework of this book. It acknowledges God (implicitly as Creator), it expresses thanks in the context of worship, it acknowledges that the world is given to humankind and the consequent need for care of it, and it sets out the purpose of that gift—so that all may enjoy the bounty of Creation.

This underlines the fact that stewardship of creation is not the same as environmental or resource stewardship. First, creation implies a Creator, and the human steward is appointed by him and responsible to him for all of creation. We most fundamentally are able to be grateful to him for the creation we enjoy! Receiving the gift has implications for fully and properly using it in line with the intentions of the Giver. Environmental stewardship may be simply a secular construct in the context of sustainable development and resource stewardship simply a variant of exploiting minerals and energy. Secondly, creation is broader than 'the environment' as normally referred to, broader than mere resources and broader even than nature[2]—the observable biosphere. It includes all God's provision for people, and hence our human stewardship must have a strongly utilitarian aspect coupled with respect and thanks.

I have already suggested that in essence, stewardship is the wise and active management of what has been abundantly provided for humankind by a loving Creator. It therefore involves discerning or assuming his general purposes in relation to that creation, starting with Scripture and applying a good measure of common sense to arrive at a qualified form of 'sustainable development'.

Understanding Creation

The starting point for faithful stewardship is an attempt to understand the Creator's view about his purposes for creation, and from that understanding the role of a steward.[3] Given the human penchant for claiming all sorts of strange ideas including hideous injustices as 'God's will', this is perhaps not a very useful observation. But we do have an evolving consensus regarding God's priorities in the world, expressed for instance in the Lausanne Statement,[4] which stresses the importance of considering the physical needs of people alongside their spiritual needs. This is relevant to the question of how we view, care for and utilise the whole of creation. Consideration of those physical needs takes us to the notion of God as Provider in his creation and to a qualified utilitarian view of it. And in contrast to the 1960s, it is now hard to find Christians who do not have an appreciation of the environment and share a concern for it,[5] so beating that drum is no longer as important as it might have been even a decade ago.

The background to this whole discussion is well known and need not be rehearsed in detail here. Realisation that careless development was having damaging effects on the environment grew strongly in the three decades from about 1965. In this context Christianity was attacked for being too anthropocentric, and interpreting God's commission in Genesis 1 to 'have dominion' as a licence to deal in a reckless, cavalier and exploitive fashion with the environment.[6] While there may be some justice in the accusation, the consensus seems to be that the root causes of environmental problems lie elsewhere, in greed and neglect, rather than simply reading 'dominion' as meaning callous 'domination'. Alister McGrath lays the blame squarely on secular attitudes arising from the Enlightenment, allowing careless and unconscionable degradation of the environment.)[7]

Paul Collins, a Catholic priest and historian, sees anthropocentrism—'the belief that we are the final purpose of the cosmos'—as the basic problem in relation to human stewardship of the environment.[8] 'It is the unconscious assumption that the Earth exists simply for humankind and that its total meaning and entire value is derived from us.' Similarly, the biologist Charles Birch[9] speaks of a 'consensus that the anthropocentric ethic, understood as an emphasis on human well-being at the expense of the Earth and other living beings, must be replaced by an ethic of respect for life and environment.' Christians could hardly take strong exception to this as stated, but to what extent are these, in the context of Christian thought and understanding, putting forward a straw man? So much of the discussion has proceeded on the basis of caricatures or at least overstatements.

The thrust of this chapter is to establish the theological basis of a balance between respect for biodiversity and 'the environment' on the one hand and respect for God's purposes vis á vis people on the other, while steering clear of the kind of anthropocentrism just defined.

'The Earth is the Lord's, and everything in it, the world and all who live in it' (Ps 24:1) is the starting point for considering our stewardship and God's purposes.

God's creation is repeatedly said to be 'good' in the Genesis 1 creation account, though the power of this is diminished in English where the word is common. In the Old Testament 'good' is preeminently an attribute of God.[10] It implies an inherent or intrinsic value which does not require any useful dimension or purpose, and establishes an obligation for us to respect it. Creation in relation to God is worthy and reveals his character: 'The heavens proclaim his righteousness and all the people see his glory' (Ps 97:6). There is abundant testimony to nature revealing God the creator as worthy to be worshipped, and in fact calling forth that worship.[11]

The final part of creation, and completing it, is humankind—created from the Earth in God's own image. Unsurprisingly the completed creation is then also said to be 'good'. Humans are the pinnacle and rulers of his creation (also Ps 8:6-8), so can never be portrayed as merely incidental to, or a pest in, the biosphere[12] as is fashionable in some quarters. But if the steward is in God's image, he/she needs to behave and discharge responsibilities accordingly; the faithful steward is expected to reflect God's character. Also, it means that a utilitarian dimension of stewardship to serve the needs of people must be taken seriously as an expression of both God's love and his purpose.[13]

Both these dimensions must be understood with all the wisdom we can bring to bear. For a start they can never be allowed to mean that we, made in God's image, treat God's creation with any less respect than he does.[14] But secondly it also means that meeting the needs of all humans, made in God's image, must be a very high priority. Environmental concern must not displace our mediation of God's provision.

Stewards of Creation

While we can be very definite in saying that stewardship involves accountability to God as Creator and as one who claims the right to be Lord in people's lives, it leaves us with the need to work out the right course of action on particular matters. But Genesis 1:28, 'Be fruitful and increase in number, fill the Earth and subdue it, rule over [every creature]' in the context of humans being made in his image clearly means an active and not merely passive role for us. The following verse (Gen 1:29) is then the first to point to the purpose of creation in providing for human needs—the plants 'will be yours for food'.

This is underlined when we get to the garden (Gen 2:8,15, in the second creation account). 'The Lord God took the man and put him in the Garden of Eden to work it and take care of it.' That is a fair summary of our commission as servant stewards, while being fruitful and increasing in numbers to 'fill the Earth' (as we certainly have). The balance between 'working' and 'taking care of'

God's creation is of course the issue addressed by this book, but both are expressions of worship.[15]

The steward role has frequently been seen as having priestly dimensions, so that human use of and care for creation is sacramental, expressing the Creator's sustaining relationship with us. The notion can certainly deepen the sense of accountability and need for care, but I would see the main priestly function as mediating and making accessible God's bounty to the needs of wider humanity.[16] The Psalmist reiterates that the maker of heaven and Earth has given the Earth to man as a blessing, leading to human expression of praise (Ps 115:15-16).

This is given further weight by the Christian understanding that Jesus as the Word 'was with God in the beginning. Through him all things were made', while Paul in his letter to the Colossians affirms of Christ that 'all things were created by him and for him. In him all things hold together',[17] so faithful discipleship affirms that everything in creation hangs together in him.

Certainly there is a noteworthy contrast between early Middle Eastern narratives where man is created to minister to the gods of nature, and Genesis where he is to civilise the Earth. Human dominion is a caring one, consequential upon being made in the image of God.[18] (The 'image of God' does not arise from his exercising dominion, as occasionally suggested.) We need to respect and respond to nature as carefully as we do to our own bodies.

The fall, where relationship with the Creator is broken,[19] does not change God's commission to humankind, though the whole enterprise of active stewardship changes character, to an extent that we cannot fully know. Our ability to care for creation in the way God intended is impaired and the bounty of his provision is compromised in practical respects. If the commission doesn't change though, our approach to it certainly does, as humanity loses sight of God's purposes and we assert our own values and agendas. God's role is usurped and *domination* of the Earth and its resources and environment rather than *dominion* becomes the name of the game. The image of God in humankind is compromised but not obliterated. The results all too often speak for themselves.

Technology, a salient aspect of the creativity in our image-of-God human nature, bestows a great capacity for harm arising from our fallen state, and is thus, in the eyes of some, itself tarnished and suspect.[20] It is technology which enables unrestrained exploitiveness. It can also contribute to an arrogance towards nature.[21] This then gives some Christians such a jaundiced view of technology that they disparage its role in stewardship and blinds them to much of God's provision through it (see later sections). Of course both theologically and practically, every good gift has the potential for abuse, or at least it represents risk.

The fall necessitates the Law, epitomised in the Ten Commandments, including such provisions as property rights which have implications for stewardship of resources and the environment (see section below on Sustainable Stewardship).

The results of the Fall are not simply in us—Genesis 3 refers to the ground being cursed at least in some agricultural sense (though it seems that God relents in Genesis 8, after the flood). Then in Genesis 6, due uniquely to human sin, God resolves to destroy his creation—not only humankind but also the other creatures, this being averted only by his provision through Noah. The Noahic covenant was explicitly with 'every living creature on Earth' (Gen 9:10) as well as Noah and his sons. Today as we see creation in its present condition, we perceive that it in itself is somehow profoundly affected—subject to frustration now but expected to be liberated from the bondage to decay (Rom 8:20-21). This anticipated cosmic redemption extends to all aspects of creation, which underlines yet again the need to respect all of it. There is no suggestion that our stewardship of it becomes futile or pointless however, nor that we can somehow expect to reverse the effects of the Fall by our own efforts. But our task and the responsibility is certainly fraught.

Theology of Creation and Romanticism

Within what is broadly called 'Christian' today we have a range of identifiable views on how God relates to his creation.

These views range from the effectively pantheist—identifying God with his creation which is therefore to be worshipped, through panentheist—with all of creation part of the divine but contingent upon the Creator, to the traditional Christian position where the creation is distinct from but reveals something important about a transcendent Creator (Rom 1:20). Pantheism excludes any notion of contingency, where creation reflects the fact that God by his divine will is both Creator and sovereign. It includes the notion of the Earth as mother, and many variants of this.[22]

Panentheism is expressed in terms of the world (or cosmos) being God's body, and God being incarnate in his creation[23] in the same sense that he is incarnate in Christ, or 'the world is essential to God, but God is not reducible to the world.'[24] In this view, sin is essentially or substantially against the world, by refusing to take responsibility or to be part of the body, rather than the traditional notion of being in rebellion against God the Father or monarch. 'If the world is God's body, then to destroy part of the world is actually to destroy part of the body of God.'[25] The Eastern Orthodox churches have tended towards a panentheist position on account of their perception of Christ's incarnation as leading to the deification of the entire cosmos. This has also received impetus from Teilhard de Chardin.[26]

A more substantial theologian at the orthodox end of the panentheist spectrum (and generally seen as mainstream) is Jürgen Moltmann. He is motivated by what he sees as the 'apocalyptic' nature of the environmental crisis. His theology[27] in this regard centres on the Holy Spirit dwelling in all of creation, which thus defines its goal and future so that 'we ultimately arrive at the transfiguring indwelling of the triune God in his creation'. The 'consummation (of that creation) will be to become the home and dwelling place of God's glory.' Moltmann steps away from what he calls an antithesis between God and the world to 'an immanent tension in God himself: God creates the world, and at the same time enters into it. He calls it into existence and at the same time manifests himself through its being. It lives from his creative power, and yet he lives in it.' It is a helpful modern exposition of God's immanence in his creation.

Panentheism is generally the position of the process theologians, who emphasise God's openness to change and identification with the events of this world. Berry points out that this features in many World Council of Churches publications[28]. Panentheism is inimical to any utilitarian understanding of creation—that it is intended to benefit people and supply resources for them.

One end of the ecofeminist spectrum is also an expression of Christian panentheism, with immanence seen as truly feminine and distinct from managerial transcendence.[29]

A particular panentheist manifestation today seems to be the Christian embrace of classical Romanticism (or at least a neo-romanticism), where 'nature' is understood metaphysically and has spiritual values which are intrinsic and not derived from a Creator. Originally, in the 18th century, Romanticism displaced Christianity to some degree in many people's world view, and they effectively saw nature (as distinct from humans) as divine, albeit within a Western context. McGrath refers to nature then being seen 'as the moral and spiritual educator of humanity,' which is an active participant in nature. 'Where science and capitalism mislead and destroy, nature leads its followers onward to personal fulfilment and integrity.'[30]

The classical Romantic view of nature as somehow sacred, and literally enchanted, does not have theological support. In fact it is essentially pagan[31], though theistic derivatives of it are widespread. Harmony with nature becomes the prime virtue, rather than a proper corollary of harmony with the Creator. As outlined in the Introduction, this view asserts a metaphysical view of nature over against science and tends to oppose any alteration to nature, not on the basis of human moral failing or fallibility, but on the basis of an idealised, pantheistic and ultimately idolatrous view of it.[32] It also shies away from grappling with any implications of God's provision in creation for people's needs, perhaps because it arises in a culture where we take for granted that no thought or effort is needed for those needs to be supplied abundantly.

Nevertheless, many of us can readily identify with today's Green Romanticism because of our own spiritual experience of nature, or of God through our experience of nature.[33] This identification from a traditional Christian perspective seems to be what has created a sort of panentheist version of it. For me, experience of nature and learning about its creatures provided the earliest and most powerful stimuli to worship God, and still I find the greatest recreational refreshment in relatively unspoiled nature. For me (as I listen to Beethoven's violin concerto while writing this), music is the only comparable stimulus—a second-order but nevertheless God-origin creation.

When Job was greatly distressed and groping for some sense of God's purpose and meaning, God spoke to him in terms of creation (Job 38-41) and God's initiative in that. His point is clear, to consider creation and develop some understanding of it is to begin to under-stand God himself. This extended lecture on natural history points to God's sovereignty and power, and draws a response of faith and repentance from Job. Does our appreciation of God's creation have a similar effect?

The modern neo-romanticism is an essentially religious attitude which largely drives parts of the environmental movement[34]. It brings a strong visceral commitment to renewable energy sources (regardless of how little they might deliver), a yearning for some sense of being connected with the land, and perhaps eco-spiritual-ity. 'Nature is a favourite site of spiritual renewal because nature is not made by human hands, and provides a sense of solidity which transcends the merely human. [In this new search for what is real], youth is instinctively drawn towards eco-spiritualty.'[35]

Outside of the Christian context, neo-romanticism may be manifest as deep ecology, a metaphysical world view which reacts against any utilitarian view of nature (which is sacred) and against anthropocentrism. Rather it is biocentric (or ecocentric) and asserts the equal value of all organisms.[36] Sometimes today this is combined with a dose of eastern mysticism or animism.

A couple of years ago I was doing my duty as a long-standing member of Australia's main conservation organisation and reading the CVs of eleven candidates who were standing for election to positions on its governing council. One read, in part: 'He is a spiritual man with deep compassion for sister bee and brother bird, and feels that it is a very special time to be on mother Earth in a climate of most wondrous continuous change.' This particular person had worked in management with DuPont, Shell, a major bank, as well as federal and state governments and the Anti-Cancer Council, before becoming head of an 'Ethical Investment' trust. His CV expressed a convergence of the Romantic and the mainstream.

Of course Christian thinkers have given great impetus to this neo-romantic perception of the environment, C. S. Lewis[37] and J. R. R. Tolkien[38] being two, though it must be noted that they wrote in a quite different era of environmental awareness. Neo-romanticism readily flourishes in a modern urban society, because so many people have lost sight of the origins of timber, metals, energy, food (and even the oxygen they breathe). So when any practical aspects of obtaining such commodities is beaten up in the media and featured in gory technicolour on our TV screens we can muster limitless indignation without the slightest thought for the wider principles or practical issues involved.

A thorough treatment of different approaches is presented in Michael Northcott's *The Environment and Christian Ethics* (1996). He distinguishes three broad approaches taken in the flowering of ecotheology—Humanocentric, Theocentric and Ecocentric, though some writers at different times fall into different categories.[39] Northcott affirms the Hebrew Bible as a sound basis for Christian ethics in relation to the environment and says that 'the non-human world as a created order is redolent of the purposes and providence of the creator God, though it is ontologically distinct from the being of God.'

The 'providence of God' in Christian writing and theology is normally applied to the understanding of God's sustaining and directing his creation, rather than drawing attention to the purpose and liberality of his provision, which is the emphasis most needed in the present discussion. God as Provider is a powerful biblical concept extending from Genesis 1 through to the New Testament, focused in his covenant people but not exclusive to them. It needs to be reasserted today as the international UN-supported environmental agenda launched in Rio de Janiero in 1992 comes around to addressing poverty and development, as it did at the World Conference on Sustainable Development in Johannesburg in 2002.

The Role of Science[40]

A corollary of perceiving the world as God's creation is that we need to understand it better and that acquiring such understanding may even be an activity of worship. This is the fundamental justification of science for Christians, though utilitarian justification need not be far behind, as expounded more fully in later chapters.

Learning about God and his creation has become fraught for some Christians in recent decades due to confusion about science's relationship to Scripture. We need to understand that the God who reveals himself in Christ and through Scripture is the same One who created the world and us. Consequently there can be no intrinsic contradiction or inconsistency in what we learn about him and his creation from whatever sources. If there seems to be, we need to review our interpretation of the evidence. While taking the Bible seriously, we must also take God's creation seriously. If we take creation seriously, we must take science seriously in exploring that creation which God delights in[41] and in mediating its provision to people.

Saint Paul reminded us that God revealed himself substantially through the natural world itself,[42] though Paul was instrumental in supplementing Old Testament and gospels to give us a much more definitive and accessible means of knowing God and his purposes. Nevertheless, his words point to the congruence between knowledge of God and knowledge of his creation—and hence science.

Science has historically to a large extent grown out of a Christian understanding of the relationship between God and his creation. The many scientists active both in research and its application who profess faith in Christ underline that relationship between special revelation in Scripture and general revelation in nature,[43] and reassure us that Truth can be sought anywhere in God's works and words. We must never be drawn into a schizophrenic notion of truth, in which people feel they need to make a choice between truth and faith, a modern echo of what Galileo was called upon to do in the 17th century.[44]

Science is a fundamental human endeavour which is implicit in our relationship, set up by God, with his created order. 'Knowledge

Science in Relation to God's Creation

We are interpreters of creation and learn from studying it that it is old and that it has changed greatly over time.[47] It is vital for Christians to have a right understanding of science, because to settle for less dishonours God and shows contempt for his creation. That is why the whole 'creation science' controversy is important.[48] Ultimately shonky science is as much of a problem as shonky theology. Denying clear scientific evidence is as silly as a Christian denying the divinity of Christ. As to what is established and what may be speculative within science, sometimes a good test is whether it works. The fact that we use numerous technologies which work reliably suggests that the science on which they are based represents a true understanding of God's creation. This however does not stop 'creation science' advocates from sending me e-mails to explain why they disdain and reject large slabs of science upon which that technology depends! Young-Earth 'creation science' also implicitly asserts that God is deceitful, having built into his work of creation conclusive evidence of a 4-5 billion year age of the Earth but expecting us to believe that it is only about 10,000 years old. A good deal of manipulation and misrepresentation of scientific evidence is required to make the case.

Scientific investigation should be pursued by appropriate methods of rational inquiry. It needs to be approached without any presuppositions of the truth or falsity of scientific theories even if some purport to be based on particular interpretations of Scripture. Science proceeds on the presupposition of order, of all truth being consistent. Such an approach to science (and in fact to general revelation) represents an application of the 'dominion' mandate given to humankind in Genesis 1 & 2. General and special revelation are complementary, as God is the author of all truth and there is no reason for us to feel threatened by truth determined in this way. This extends to theories of cosmological and biological evolution as well as to other aspects of scientific inquiry. As noted above, it means that if information from scientific inquiry appears to be inconsistent with a particular interpretation of Scripture, then it is necessary to look more closely at both sources rather than manipulating the data.[49]

'Creation science', asserting a 6-day creation some 10,000 years ago, is founded on the misreading of a metaphor (not to mention taking it out of the context of the parallel account in Genesis 2).[50] It is fundamentally a hermeneutical aberration,[51] which then forces preconceptions and consequent distortion on the scientific theorising of those involved.[52] So while 'creation science' does not declare itself as anti-scientific, it subverts proper science as does its new manifestation: Intelligent Design. Intelligent Design attacks particular scientific positions on the grounds that if there is a scientific explanation there is no room for God to be at work, which is a complete misunderstanding of both creation and the scientific approach to understanding it. Both are often expressed as a brand of fundamentalism[53] where new truth is intolerable and not allowed to stand in the way of sincere religious zeal. But the same zeal can readily be expressed within a framework of understanding that God's revelation in Scripture and science are complementary, without the closed mind which rejects much of what the mind is created for.

is the characteristically human way of participating in the cosmic order', as O'Donovan[45] has put it. Professor Graeme Clarke goes further. In listing many distinguished scientists and mathematicians who were committed Christians he asserts that 'their Christian faith led them to the truth they uncovered'. Certainly this is true in his own case, leading the team which against great odds developed the 'bionic ear' (cochlear implant).[46]

Science is vital to our understanding of creation and informing our stewardship of it (see box).

Applying the resources of the Earth to human need for an ever-increasing population is a clear human priority, one which is discussed further in the next section. The technology for this is based on the science which gives us an insight into the working of God's creation.[54] Both the science and the technology are derivative from his creation—the world with its natural resources and humankind with our inbuilt intellectual resources. Technology has long been understood in the Reformed tradition as a tool of stewardship in the service of God.[55] As the human demands on God's provision increase, applying our God-given gifts in developing and deploying technology in the service of humankind becomes ever more essential.[56]

However, science can never be divorced from those who practice and champion it. Some scientists are notorious in speaking well beyond their competence, which does not help credibility of science as a whole, though such occasions are usually discernible. More seriously, there have been occasions when scientists have boosted their discoveries in the public arena unreasonably, or given reassurance where it was unwarranted, and this has caused scepticism when the facts prove to fall short of the hype. Then problems of credibility arise when scientists speak out on other issues. While a little scepticism is healthy, disparagement of science as a result of these occasions is not.

The other obvious problem with the application of science through technology has been referred to earlier in the chapter —the tendency to develop an anthropocentric hubris. This was possibly most evident in the policies of the former Soviet Union and delivered more and greater environmental disasters than any regime in history—the Chernobyl accident being the best known.[57]

God's revelation in Scripture and in Christ touch specifically upon both natural resources and human intellectual resources to a very limited extent. Nevertheless, science, technology and economics (which has elements of both science and technology) are natural and appropriate human activities for those made in God's image and put in charge of all that he has provided. They need to be applied ethically and with wisdom. We are his co-workers, and in a distinctly subsidiary sense, even his co-creators through applying technology. God's creative presence in the world is open-ended and emergent, so humankind 'can exercise his created creativity consciously in cooperation with the Creator'.[58] Of course this extends also to the arts, where the Spirit works through people most wonderfully, whether or not they acknowledge the source of their creativity.

So we are never more fully human, in God's image,[59] than when we are exploring his creation to understand it better and then applying the fruits of that scientific understanding through technology to address human needs, (unless perhaps in exploring all of his revelation in order to worship him?). Obviously this must not be a utilitarianism divorced from an appreciation of God's transcendence and love, but an appropriate worship of that creator God, accompanied by respect for his creation. It is thus distinguished from science as scientism—a secular ideology and world view.[60]

In passing, we can note that modern science and technology have arisen in a Christian, and particularly post-Reformation, cultural context and arguably owe their success to that. In this regard, Denis Alexander has a magnificent account of science-faith issues in *Rebuilding the Matrix* (2001). While to some degree science and technology have emerged in other cultures such as Chinese and Arabic well before the Christian Reformation, outside of the Christian context for a variety of reasons they did not lead anywhere, and died out.

God's provision:
Sustainable stewardship as care and use

The earliest human activity recorded in Genesis (2:18-20) is naming the animals (specifically all the beasts and birds). While the purpose of this was evidently social, it is clear that a fundamental aspect of human relationship with the rest of creation is to be found in this activity of recognition and naming. He who bestows names has authority to do so and also he enters into a relationship with the creatures he names. And, just as a difference in appreciation may be discerned in human relationships where a name is used instead of an impersonal pronoun or generic noun, so here. Today this same appreciation is expressed not simply by taxonomists (who might arguably be Adam's successors in naming!) but by the bird watchers, field naturalists and others who enjoy discovering and learning about the creatures around us. 'Great are the works of the Lord, studied by all who delight in them'.[61]

Stewardship of the created world involves both caring for it as God's handiwork, respecting and admiring it, but also with thanks and rejoicing[62] making its bounty accessible to the six billion people whom God loves. Especially is this true for the least well-off 2-3 billion—those inconvenient statistics (for many environmentalists) each of whom is person made in God's image. One reason this is so hard for us is that we tend to be hung up on a 'Limits to Growth' kind of concept about scarcity of resources, whereas closer consideration would leave us amazed that they are so abundant, as one would expect from a generous God. A great deal of work is called for on our part to realise and make available that abundance on a sustainable basis and avoid polluting it, but the limits are ours, not his, as the following chapters make clear. Broadly speaking, when has any human activity or legitimate aspiration ever been limited by any shortcoming on God's provision for us? When is it ever likely to be?[63]

The Gaia hypothesis put forward by James Lovelock[64] should be mentioned here. It arises from the notion of a 'balance of nature' and represents the Earth and its atmosphere—organisms and their material environment—as a self-regulating system with complex

climate and chemistry feedbacks which maintain conditions
for life. It countered the then prevalent scientific reductionism,
included humanity with nature, and has gained significant scientific support as it has evolved. It suggests the metaphor of 'a living
Earth' and here it transcends the boundary of the metaphysical in
some respects and attracts support from distinctly non-scientific
environmentalists. These extend it to view the Earth as essentially
'a living creature which can be abused or propitiated', or even 'a
divine entity to be worshipped as a goddess from whose womb we
have come'.[65] The original concept suggests the need for care in the
context of use, but is sometimes treated with some reservation by
Christians because it has echoes of Earth religions and New Age
spirituality and has been adopted to become the scientific basis of
pantheistic deep ecology.[66]

Today there is much rhetoric on the issue of sustainability and
sustainable development.[67] Beyond the obvious, this acquires
various meanings according to the source and context under
consideration. It is sometimes a very slippery notion, but here I
take primarily the plain English meaning, and apply it in a relative
rather than absolute sense, to seek policies which are more sustainable than others. Certainly sustainability is the overriding principle
of today's environmental concern and it is also finding its way
into corporate rhetoric about the wider responsibilities of modern
business,[68] where it has three legs: economic, environmental and
social.

It would be hard to find anyone to disagree with the notion that
land use and resource use, including energy, needs to be sustainable and not merely undertaken with regard to short-term interests.
Sustainability may include consideration of how substantial is
the resource base, and how accessible it is in the light of possible
political developments. It also includes safety, risks, affordability,
and the need for minimising environmental effects (ie wastes must
be manageable and costed in).

In his *God's Book of Works*, Professor Berry[69] sets out Ten
Premises for Sustainable Living, helpfully drawing together the key
ethical and practical elements of several major international pro-
nouncements up to 1992. He says that the Ten Premises 'represent

a convergence of ideas describing the whole nature, properties and management of the Earth' and hopes that they might provide the same kind of 'focus for sustainable development .... as does Darwinian theory for biology'. While helpfully steering away from rights language the Ten Premises, like their precursors, are almost totally environmental and barely include resource access and equity. They do not reflect the more recent emphasis in sustainable development to alleviation of poverty as expressed at the 2002 World Conference on Sustainable Development held in Johannesburg. We need more attention on how resources and energy are accessed, their equitable development and distribution, and how widespread poverty can be overcome sustainably.

In considering the balance between care and use of God's creation, there is the question of what is now called intergenerational equity—a fundamental principle of sustainable development, and one which is congenial to Christian concerns. Our stewardship must serve not only this, but subsequent generations, and ensure that their options are not unduly limited because of our actions. However, having said this we need to note the propensity for advocates of intergenerational concerns having hidden agendas,[70] though this tends to be only slightly less obvious than elsewhere in environmental debates.

Intergenerational equity is one obvious subset of sustainability, but equity within this generation and especially internationally is no less important though until recently it has not been high profile in the sustainability context.

So there is a wide range of criteria, which makes sustainability, or sustainable development (in terms of the UN World Commission on Environment and Development) a useful ethical umbrella for environmental discourse. It can readily bring together Christian priorities of sustainable stewardship with wider societal values. For instance, Professor Berry[71] identifies a convergence over the last two or three decades between public concerns expressed politically and Christian notions of stewardship of the world, which seems to be leading to 'a truly natural theology' simply because we are having to come to terms with reality. 'The nature and properties of creation are such that certain features are appearing that determine (or prescribe) a proper treatment for it.' This points us 'to the credibility of ... God, and the coherence between his special and general revelations'.

An aspect of the stewardship of God's creation, and one fundamental to the sustainability of that stewardship, is economic. The creation of wealth by saving and investment goes hand in hand with the development and use of technology in making God's provision available to the people on Earth. That wealth creation is broader than simply financial—it includes all the material aspects, together with human skills and knowledge in a civilisation. Without wealth creation, leading to further investment, technology would remain rudimentary, and the support of six billion people would be impossible.[72] Improving the living conditions of the poorest two billion would be simply a fantasy.

Like technology, wealth creation is tainted by the fact that fallen humans pursue it selfishly and sometimes perversely. We even have bizarre Christian aberrations such as prosperity doctrine,[73] arising from a profound misunderstanding of God's grace. But though it requires individual decision and sacrifice of consumption, wealth is not simply an individual concept. People need to work together cooperatively to create wealth, and trade is fundamental. It is at the level of common wealth that whole societies can escape poverty and move from subsistence towards a standard of living that many of us happily take for granted. The mechanism of saving and investment, and the accumulation of capital and infrastructure, is too obvious to require extended comment here. Its importance can be gauged by comparing any Western society with those where common wealth in some form has not been created and accumulated.[74]

Moving from the hunter-gatherer level of existence to agriculture involved the first step in wealth creation—saving some harvested grain and later sowing it as seed for a future crop, or keeping some livestock in order to breed more or to provide produce such as milk, eggs or wool. In each case consumption was foregone to enable and create investment. The seed or the husbanded livestock became working capital which enabled more of the same in the future.

This transition appears to be part of what the new people of Israel, basking in the bounty of Canaan, are called to remember.

Moses' speech in Deuteronomy, setting out the law and reinforcing the need to remember God's saving acts, concludes with rules for offering the firstfruits and tithes. 'When you have entered the land the Lord your God is giving you as an inheritance and have taken possession of it and settled it (and started to enjoy its agricultural produce), take some of the firstfruits of all that you produce from the soil of the land' in order to express your thanks for God's provision. After going to the priest, 'you shall declare before the Lord your God: 'My father was a wandering Aramean and he went down into Egypt with a few people and lived there and became a great nation'.'[75] The incidental point here is that Abraham was a Syrian nomad, and the word translated 'wandering' in NIV is literally (as AV) 'ready to perish', pointing to the precarious nature of such pre-agricultural existence, only one step from hunter-gatherer. Nomadic life was also plainly a way of existence supporting rather fewer people than settled agricultural Canaan.

Wealth creation, like the development and application of technology, is all part of God's provision through human activity, part of what he expects us to be doing as people created in his image.[76] The 'noble savage' stereotype is a myth and has no place in a Christian understanding of how to exercise faithful stewardship of God's creation today, let alone in enabling billions of people to enjoy a healthy existence on God's Earth.

So, Christian concern needs to encourage the creation of wealth without its undue concentration or the corresponding deprivation of weaker individuals. Christians also acknowledge that God has provided very abundantly for his creatures, notably humanity, and that human organisation (such as government) needs to expedite access to this abundance, rather than diminish it.

Finally we need to face the question of limits to sustainability—are we running out of world?[77] The answer is both yes and no. Yes, humankind has always been bumping up against those limits, as we are today, and no, because we have constantly pushed them out through the activities expounded in this book, through innovation and learning from our mistakes. We will always face limits, the question is what, as faithful stewards of God's creation, we do about extending them. Whether there are absolute limits which are not amenable to being extended as described in later chapters is unknown, and as much a theological as a scientific question. Certainly the perception of looming limits has the power to alter human behaviour, and that is part and parcel of the adaptability which this book aims to draw attention to and encourage as Christian vocation.

Declaration on the Care of Creation[78]

Christian engagement with environmental issues has been belated, on the whole. It has been well shown that it is historical nonsense to blame Christianity (or Judaism) as scapegoats for environmental problems, but while the charge has a flimsy basis it has been pervasive and enduring. As noted above, there has been a strong attack from the standpoint of biocentrism to the effect that stewardship of creation is 'repulsively anthropocentric'.[79] And even in the churches, never a year goes by without some exalted cleric announcing that Christians ought to wake up to his list of new-found greenish concerns.

In 1990 the World Council of Churches addressed the need for Christian engagement with environmental issues. Unfortunately it did so in a way which eroded the proper basis of this engagement: namely, humans being made in the image of the Creator. As a result, the *Evangelical Declaration on the Care of Creation* was launched in 1994[80] to set the record straight, stake out some ground in the green agenda and guide the faithful.

Ron Sider in expounding the context points out that 'if we do not offer biblical foundations for environmental actions, we will have only ourselves to blame if environmental activists turn to other, finally inadequate, worldviews and religions'.[81] He is right in the sense that we need to do this for the benefit of many, but we cannot assume the general absence of any ideological commitment which is profoundly anti-Christian as well as being effectively opposed to the science and technology which arises out of a Christian understanding of creation.

The book *The Care of Creation*[82] later appeared, as a valuable and important collection and presentation of theological comment on the Declaration from mainstream evangelical theologians and others in various parts of the world, edited by Professor R.J. (Sam) Berry. The 18 contributions are diverse, and add up to a valuable collection bearing upon 1990s concerns and understanding of environmental issues.

The contributors cover a lot of ground very helpfully, and they are all the more valuable for each being tied to the Declaration (despite its shortcomings). The tenor is academic (most authors are Professors) rather than practical, and but for passing reference in one item they do not address how resource-accessing activities even as basic as farming should be conducted to serve the needs of people. Both the Declaration and the commentary on it are shaped by a perspective which focuses on greed, 'perverted stewardship' and a litany of environmental degradation rather than on responsibly utilising God's bounty on his Earth. Where one would expect to see a balance between utilitarian and conservation aspects expounded, we have caricatures presented as though the economic dimension of life did not exist[83] and God's provision was understood in some Garden of Eden context. There is a glaring gap in relation to the aspects of creation which we draw upon to serve human needs, and in relation to our stewardship of it to mediate or liberate God's provision for people.

The 160 core pages of the book avoid mention of industry such as mining and forestry, except by way of listing the standpoints and presumed motivation of those who attack the Declaration. We have only the park/gardening metaphor of stewardship, and even that has been divorced from anything managerial. So how, exactly, should we view the world's natural resources? How is God's provision to be understood and accessed? They are clearly part of what is entrusted to people for use[84] and our civilisation (not to mention the survival of most of the world's population) clearly depends on them. So a Christian exposition of care for creation which treats them as unmentionable is unhelpful, and underlines the need for fuller exposition of the subject.

The book makes it clear that the Declaration was forged under heavy fire from the US Christian Right (Calvin Beisner[85] being the *bete noir),* which may explain its bunkering down in the other direction. One chapter, 'The Declaration under siege', documents a slanging match where apparently neither side learns from the other. Obviously those comprising the US Christian Right are a key audience or at least a reference point for the book.

The point here is that the Declaration is not significantly wrong, but it is unbalanced and deficient in neither affirming and celebrating the Creator's provision of natural resources and the technology to utilise them, nor acknowledging the positive human steps to reduce environmental impacts in the process. The balance is not redressed in the commentary. Regrettably, it invites more of the scorn already heaped by a few on the Declaration itself, which deserves to be defended for its virtues and enhanced in relation to its shortcomings.

Several other books also present valuable insights on creation care. One of these is Steven Bouma-Prediger's book, *For the Beauty of the Earth: A Christian Vision for Creation Care* (Baker Academic, 2001). Like many others it suffers from its academic perspective devoid of any grappling with practical aspects of how to care for creation while using it as God evidently intended. Its context is not the world of agriculture, mining and forestry, but a US college where the author shows that the case for a theological approach to anything outside the church has still to be made.

The author quickly dismisses any thought of the natural world as a natural resource 'to be managed as prudently as possible by humans for human good' by packaging that thought with others and consigning them to the grossly inadequate and too anthropocentric basket (p. 128). He concludes that 'the challenge ahead is to persuade Christians that care for the Earth is an integral feature of authentic Christian discipleship' (p. 135). That may well be so in places, but for me today's challenge is to understand how to utilise resources faithfully and apply them to the real needs of real people while certainly caring for the creation of which they are a part.

It helpfully reminds us that, 'God is the rightful and proper owner of the Earth, but God gives us the calling to be earthkeepers. We are given the joy and the responsibility to lovingly keep the garden that is the Earth—in all its intricate fullness and dynamic relatedness, From this theological motif comes the ethical principle of beneficence. Doing good for the sake of the other is the essence of serving and keeping the Earth' (pp. 154-55) One wonders what the implications of substituting 'farm' for 'garden' might be! This precious attitude which ignores the 'dynamic relatedness' of the world's six billion people with the abundant provision in God's creation is staggering. In a section on 'God's concerns are our concerns' we learn that 'Christian earthkeepers are not misanthropes' (p. 177). But the author slides off the point by saying that 'This objection wrongly assumes that the gospel is somehow unconnected to the earth, ... as if our Redeemer is not our Creator.' Back to the ivory tower! It simply does not seem to have occurred to the author that our Creator might just be concerned that a few billion more people gain better access to food, resources and energy.

The environment is a contentious issue, all the more so as urban dwellers forget where God's provision of food, fibre, fuel, and other materials come from, let alone how they are extracted and processed. Christians who engage in comment on environmental issues are not helpful if they ignore these basic facts of modern life however, and the Declaration's deficiency needs attention. Green Romanticism, even if anointed by Christians, is a cop-out. Christian stewardship of creation means that we need to help one another try and perceive that creation from the Creator's perspective, and discern his purposes in all the varied and extraordinarily abundant provision he has made. We also need a sound and mature understanding of technology as a human attribute of people created in his image, as outlined in a later chapter. Then we can get a better idea of how to approach the whole creation with a coherent sense of utilitarian, aesthetic and spiritual goals.

In practical terms Christian concern must be for personal behaviour and ultimately government policy which puts these principles into effect. Some practical aspects are explored in following chapters. The human institutional aspects of stewardship—political, social and economic—occupy a short section in chapter 3.

2

Finding Space on Earth

A wealthy multinational oil company is considering part of a well-known national park to explore for what is arguably the lifeblood of our lifestyle. Many people spring to the national park's defence on the presumption that it would thereby be ruined. What should happen? Where should Christians take their stand, and why? I know what my initial reaction would be if it concerned one of the areas I and my family have enjoyed camping in regularly over the years!

Many would represent this as a clash between conservation and consumerism, respect for God's creation versus the primacy of profits. The matter may not be so simple, and it raises some major questions for those concerned with stewardship of God's creation.

Use and Non-use of Land

Land is fundamental to our human and cultural identity, even if many people today live somewhat removed from it, except perhaps for its urban relict manifestations.[1] There are degrees of use of land, from the intensive radical alteration caused by cities and roads, to agriculture of varying degrees of intensity (but at least using the soil), to grazing rangeland, to forestry which may harvest timber every few years or decades, to low-intensity hunter-gatherer or recreation use. If all of the world's inhabitants relied on hunter-gatherer use of land we would all be very hungry. It is agriculture, at increasing intensity and productivity, which enables six billion to be fed[2].

Returning to our initial dilemma and conflict, what is a national park or equivalent conservation reserve? It can be many different things, from a virgin ecosystem, perhaps wilderness, coupled with stunning scenery, to something like some UK National Parks which are largely altered by farming, mining, transport and settlement. But let's default to the undisturbed ecosystem for the sake of teasing out the principles.

Secondly, what is the national park for? Nature conservation per se? Human recreation? Some compromise mixture? A prime attribute of land, viewed from any conservation perspective, is the biodiversity it supports. Original, maximum, or undiminished biodiversity are variously taken as being good, while its diminution is bad.[3] Certainly conservation of biodiversity needs to be a default position in any concept of stewardship of God's creation.

And what is development, that so disturbs those who see themselves as guardians of such pristine tracts of the Earth's surface? It may be people pressure, assisted (or exacerbated) by improved access and accommodation, it may be forestry, it may be mining or oil exploration (with the presumption of developing a mine or oilfield if successful). Or it may be many other things which don't involve wholesale alteration. And is alteration automatically to be equated with damage? Is there moral value in naturalness? What theological principles apply? Where do practical responses to human needs come into it?

In a national park or reserve of only a few square kilometres which preserves some scenic feature or remnant vegetation, developing an open cut mine or any other significant disturbance would not be entertained, despite any credible assurance of eventual rehabilitation. Nor would ongoing clear-fell forestry on, say, an 80 year cycle. But an underground mine, with its access portal outside the park? An inconspicuous wellhead? A beekeeping enterprise? Selective logging of a single minor tree species? Access for tourists in 4WD vehicles? Hikers? Where do we draw the line? If the open cut mine or other major impact disturbs less than one unobtrusive square kilometre in a national park of 2000 square kilometres, does that make any difference? Or is such development sacrilege, or at least the thin edge of the wedge?

Aside from tactical issues and politics which tend to confuse and override rational consideration, the questions drive us either to rules or principles, and it is most useful to focus on the principles, in the context of the considerations in the previous chapter.

The first practical principle is that, under God, governments are appointed to govern on behalf of their citizens. In relation to determining which land is used for what in the context of evolving needs, this commonly involves some kind of land use planning with public input at some stage so as to ascertain and respond to the citizens' views. (It is assumed here that the ownership of minerals is on behalf of all citizens, not private, and that the government also has substantial control over, if not sometimes ownership of, the land surface in question). Flowing from this is their responsibility to ensure that all the resources—physical and other—benefit their citizens long-term.

The second principle is that land use allocation must be according to the capacity of that land for the potential use. *Prima facie*, rare attributes such as most mineral resources should have priority over common or widespread ones, such as forestry or agricultural potential, since they cannot be conjured into existence elsewhere by government (or other) fiat. And if this is not recognised, where will the minerals or whatever come from? Simply saying 'somewhere else' may move but not remove the problem, and depending on the reasons for it, may be grossly irresponsible stewardship in relation to God's provision for human needs.

Biological features or scenic splendour may be either rare or common attributes, and this tends to determine whether particular land is put into some kind of reserve well before our hypothetical conflict occurs. In any case, it is a factor in the decision-making. But in the last 30 years in some parts of the world such as Australia, some large tracts of land have been reserved with little thought about other possible uses and simply to get the national proportion of such reserves up to five percent or more. Lines are ruled on maps and thereafter deemed to represent demarcation of conservation values—they thereby determine the fate of what is unknown beneath.[4] Does such land use allocation need periodic review (e.g., every 30 years) in the light of further information—more knowledge of the land together with evolving needs and values in the community?

Stewardship of Land: Principles and Values

Stewardship of land as addressed here is a subset of human and creaturely stewardship of God's creation as a whole. This chapter gives particular attention to mining—an aspect of land use with particular (and arguably unique) difficulties and which has proved contentious in many parts of the world. Mining tends to bring the discourse down to Earth, often sharply.

What is the significance of 'land' to different people? Among other things:

• As a resource base, for growing food and other needs, and containing minerals
• Enabling biodiversity
• Essential to a sense of communal identity, as in OT and many indigenous peoples today
• As security, especially where tradable property rights exist[5]
• Giving a sense of transcendence to many modern people.[6]

What is Christian stewardship of this land? How is the concept to be understood and applied? This depends on how the Creator and owner is understood in relation to that land and to nature generally.

As noted in chapter 1, the emerging Christian consensus on the importance of considering the physical needs of people alongside their spiritual needs is relevant to the question of how we view, care for and utilise the land. If people are the pinnacle of God's creation and not merely a pest in the biosphere[7], then a utilitarian dimension of stewardship and hence land use must be taken seriously.

But today we have to grapple with the legacy of unwise utilitarian approach to land use, where agricultural development has exceeded the capacity of the land and climate to sustain it. In Australia vast areas suffer from salinity brought about either by clearing deep-rooted woody plants or by inappropriate irrigation. This will take decades to rectify and is a cautionary tale regarding ecological limits and the imperative to consider sustainability. Elsewhere soil erosion is a long-term blight and represents the antithesis of stewardship.

On the other hand, today's upsurge of the classical Romantic view of nature as somehow sacred, and literally enchanted, goes beyond any proper Christian view and particularly affects our approach to land use. This Romantic perception of the environment readily flourishes in a modern urban society, because, after all, timber comes from the hardware shop, metals come from a factory somewhere, energy is laid on all round and food is abundant at the supermarket. So we can safely protest about the despoilation of the environment by greedy companies engaged in the sordid tasks of forestry, mining, oil and gas production, and so on. On top of that, we forget that most of our food comes from wide-scale environmental rape and pillage—on any consistently applied preservationist criteria! How many improved pastures or wheat fields retain even a vestige of their original ecosystems? Agricultural land is changed radically, and if the world is to be fed we must accept that—while being careful to avoid degradation of the soil resource through erosion and salinity.

The Bible, in both teaching and anecdote, is concerned chiefly with pastoral and agricultural land uses, and a good deal is said about practical aspects of making these sustainable. By implication, due to the extolled attributes of the promised land and because of approval of their products, it supports mining and forestry[8]. There is little direct support for purely conservation uses, unless one includes the concept of wilderness. But given the importance of the link between perceiving his handiwork in creation and praising or worshipping the Creator, one hardly needs an explicit biblical warrant to place land and biological conservation as a high priority today, in an era of great population and resource use pressure in many parts of the world.

So, stewardship of land involves both caring for it as God's handiwork, respecting and admiring it, but also making its bounty sustainably accessible to the six billion people whom God loves.

Land Use and Minerals

Deciding upon land use depends on knowing its potential, and while the principle of allocating land use accordingly can be applied logically, it commonly is not, leading to controversy or even confrontation. A major problem is that while the potential of an area of land can readily be determined for most attributes in the course of a systematic land use planning process or some lesser evaluation, for minerals beneath it cannot.[9] This means that on a purely rational basis a third principle may be that access for mineral exploration should be maintained indefinitely.

This of course excites considerable opposition from preservationists and others, not without reason, since a company will only put money into exploration—a very expensive process—if there is at least some prospect of exploiting what may be found. Therefore in practice one needs to identify any areas which could never conceivably be disturbed, and then only explore if access underground could be gained from outside their bounds, which is increasingly feasible. For instance, the Olympic Dam mine in South Australia has hundreds of kilometres of drives and tunnels more than 350 metres below the surface, and it is quite conceivable that these might be say 10 km from any surface access and plant.[10] Obviously any exploration would need to be conducted with very little impact on the land surface, as it can be—and in such areas, is.

Mining has always had to grapple with the question of other land uses, because it is generally high-value and intensive, traditionally occupying only a small area, and therefore prevailing in that small area. Furthermore, minerals belong to the state in most parts of the world deriving their polity from Europe (but not in the USA), giving a further reason for mining to prevail. However, multiple land use is basic to most Mines Acts,[14] though originally this presupposed underground mining hence small surface impact.

Complementary Land Uses

Land uses of a particular area maybe multiple and complementary, or they may be exclusive. Generally, any government-mandated

Jabiluka

A current controversy in Australia is instructive, and now involves the London-based Rio Tinto company. A uranium mine, Jabiluka, has been developed but not yet actually mined. It is adjacent to the existing (25-year old) Ranger mine in the Northern Territory. Surrounding the two contiguous leases is the famous Kakadu National Park. The Park and the mining leases are both Aboriginal land. Following a full environmental assessment process, Jabiluka has government approval to proceed but is vehemently opposed by many environmentalists and a number of the Aboriginal traditional owners. The latter have genuine concerns about social issues arising from development in the region, including tourism, mining impacts and even Park management, but are also much influenced (some would say, manipulated) by environmentalists. Those traditional owners are exercising a minor but economically significant veto. Other Aboriginals involved are keen to see the mine proceed, not least for its broad financial benefits in the region and the positive social programs that it would enable to continue and develop after Ranger closes. This appears like a classic case of development threatening to trample over nature and indigenous peoples, and some work hard to portray it thus.

But there is a history to this, and failure to understand that raises some serious ethical issues. In 1969-70 a number of uranium orebodies[11] including Ranger and Jabiluka were discovered in this region. By the mid 1970s there were also proposals to create a large national park in the area. In 1975 the federal government commissioned a major public Inquiry, which reported two years later that uranium development could proceed here if certain measures were taken. The government adopted most of the Inquiry's recommendations. Three mining leases encompassed four orebodies and these were excluded from the Kakadu National Park as it was progressively set up. (Other orebodies were relinquished to the Park due to their particular locations, and thereby written off.) The National Park is now 19,800 square kilometres, about the size of Israel or half the size of Switzerland.

The present senior traditional owner inherited from her father the agreement to develop Jabiluka but now disagrees with it, despite the fact that she was one of a group of five Aboriginal traditional owners who lobbied the federal Labor government in 1991 to allow Jabiluka to proceed. Situated on a 73 square kilometre lease, the mine itself would be one of the world's largest in terms of uranium ore reserves accessed (its uranium would make enough electricity to supply the whole UK for about eight years). It would involve disturbing about 80 hectares of land including the area required for a road, be out of sight of tourists, and the area would be subsequently rehabilitated (with the government holding a bond sufficient to fund this). After this the (mostly undisturbed) mining lease area would be added to the National Park. In December 2000, UNESCO's World Heritage Centre concluded 'that the currently approved proposal for the mine and mill at Jabiluka[12] does not threaten the health of the people or the biological and ecological systems of Kakadu National Park.'

So what principles does the Christian apply here? Government sovereignty, due process, clear mining company title and the capacity of the land all point strongly to mining. But public sentiment in the major cities today is against it, partly due to prejudice regarding uranium, partly due to the perception that Jabiluka is 'in' Kakadu National Park — a major conservation icon, and partly out of sympathy for those Aboriginal traditional owners who currently oppose it. Should this sentiment prevail over due process, economic values and the property rights of the mining company (which has invested some $200 million in the project so far)? If so, do we support the notion that any development or title can properly and ethically be nullified by an energetic public campaign of opposition which presses the right buttons of public sentiment?[13] If not, is due process inexorable, immune from review and impervious to public opinion? Wherein does faithful stewardship lie?

land use which excludes other uses is a simple bureaucratic solution to a complex problem.

National parks commonly exclude specified developments, for instance. The question of whether they need or should do so is another matter, and in the UK it is noteworthy that a good deal more latitude is taken for granted than in USA and Australia

This raises the question of values—both intrinsic in the land as it is found, and those related to how it is used. Nature conservation values are asserted by some as necessarily pre-eminent, while others see development and economic return as taking precedence, and indeed, an ethical imperative. Both views may appeal to Christian principles in support. The former may assert that any national park or equivalent reserve is automatically incommensurable, and putting any development in it would be like cutting holes in the Mona Lisa. This is essentially a moral position which places a paramount value on avoiding change, or at least that induced rapidly by human action.

But, in relation to the citizens and their government which set it up and maintains it, what is a national park for? Apart from any objective nature conservation purpose which can be achieved through scientifically-informed management, is it so that citizens can feel good that some element of their land is preserved, even though they may never visit it from their urban bedlam? Is it so that visitors might have a wilderness experience, reconnecting with nature (or Nature) and perhaps meet God there?

Where does a perspective rooted in a sense of Christian stewardship of God's creation lead us with our national park? Or other land? To Green Romanticism, resisting the inroads of human (especially technological) influence? Or to unrestrained exploitation of the Earth's resources? If some balance of minimum disturbance with utilisation for human benefit, how is it arrived at? Practically, politically or ideologically?

Even if we respect the land as part of nature which is God's handiwork, we have seen that that handiwork is expressed in both the beauty of the place and the usefulness of the resources he has created, not just one without the other. We have no alternative but to work out and somehow agree how much beauty we allow to be disturbed and to risk, and how much priority to give to accessing the natural resources to fuel our economy. Our forebears cleared vast areas of forests to make farms, we may therefore give higher priority to maintaining the forests that remain. But should this be as commercial sources of timber and wood fibre (on a sustainable basis) or as national parks? And if, employing sound ecological principles, we can achieve two objectives at once—largely if not absolutely, should we as stewards do so? I suggest so.

One particular issue which is now arising in many parts of the world is the burial and disposal of wastes. Obviously this can be an 'out of sight, out of mind' procedure without professional care (as many case studies testify), or it may be undertaken in such a way that the wastes (as solids) are secure from disturbance or being mobilised and do not affect subsequent (possibly restricted) surface uses. A particular subset of this is burial or deep geological disposal[15] of radioactive wastes. In the case of Yucca Mountain in Nevada, USA, some US$ 5 billion has been spent on simply assessing a particular site for its suitability for secure geological disposal of all the US high-level radioactive waste (mostly spent reactor fuel)! It is rightly assumed that people will want safe access to the land surface indefinitely, and disposal plans take this into account.

Radioactive waste disposal is a subject in itself, but in relation to this chapter I simply remark that it would be good if anything like the same scruples applied to other toxic wastes which do not have the emotive force or the pay-as-you-go funding (in the case of civil spent fuel). The stewardship considerations involved with wastes go back to how they are generated and to ensuring long-term safety of their disposal. From a green Romantic perspective of course all waste disposal into the bowels of the Earth is an insult and violation, and where any alternative is proffered it is indefinite supervised storage on the surface—hardly compatible with the intergenerational equity aspect of stewardship. This aversion to deep geological disposal is all the more strange when one remembers that the heat of the Earth's core is maintained by radioactive decay already, so placing long-lived radioactive wastes deep into the Earth's crust has a certain geological appropriateness. Also its safety case is supported by the evidence of 'wastes' from the several natural nuclear reactors which operated in water-soaked uranium deposits about two billion years ago, in what is now west Africa. Those wastes moved only a few metres, with none of the technological impediments to such mobility which are now required and taken for granted.[16]

So, if significant land uses can be complementary, is that *prima facie* better stewardship than asserting one to the exclusion of the other? In particular, if oil development or mining can take place without affecting the nature conservation values or the nature experience of visitors or the aesthetics of a national park, then should it be allowed? If it affects both but only in very restricted areas, should it be allowed? Are the compromises to be worked out in territorial disputes over contested hectares, or in the more intelligent management of larger areas? Which kind of compromise is most appropriate in stewardship of each part of the whole creation?

More broadly, if we fail to embrace the principle of complementary land uses, are we likely eventually to create artificial shortages which are not part of God's plan and cut across his generous provision for humanity? Faithful stewardship is fraught with hard decisions.

Wilderness

While the British Romanticism idealised essentially artificial landscapes, in the USA and subsequently Australia, attention was focused on pristine forests and other landscapes which could be described as wilderness.[17] As well as being unspoiled, these areas have the characteristic of being people-free, and that aspect has become defining. They are also associated with spiritual quest.

The Sierra Club was founded in the USA in 1892 on a strongly wilderness-oriented basis fostered by John Muir, though it was Aldo Leopold in 1926 who secured the first US reservation of a designated wilderness area.[18] It was Leopold who put forward the notion of a land ethic, complementing personal and social ethics.[19] In Australia the first effectively wilderness national parks were proclaimed a few years earlier.[20] In all this, wilderness was seen as preserving a scientifically-important remnant of original ecosystems for human study but it was most of all promoted to fill the emotional needs of an increasingly-urbanised society, helping it stay in touch with its primitive roots. Others speak of the spiritual impact of wilderness, enabling or causing better understanding of the individual's self and of humanity's relationship with Nature.[21]

There are several problems with the notion of wilderness however. First, it cannot be assumed that wilderness areas are as devoid of historic human influence as usually asserted, nor that they need any less management than other national park areas. Secondly, there is the current question of aboriginal occupation, access and use which cuts across such reservation based on the felt needs of urbanised people. The dilemma faced by John Muir in the USA 110 years ago is much the same as in many parts of Australia, Africa and South America today. Wilderness (and indeed much of the national park area in Australia and USA) is essentially non-utilitarian and is promoted on an ecocentric moral basis, but traditional rights of native people do not generally respect this, nor *vice versa*.

In some cases, native people are excluded or expelled from wilderness to preserve its sanctity. In April 2002 the Bushmen of Kalahari, Africa's last nomadic people, lost a legal battle against being evicted from their homeland by the Botswana government. The Central Kalahari Game Reserve was originally set up in 1961 by the British to provide a refuge for both the Bushmen and wildlife. The present government wants to focus on the wildlife and has resettled the Bushmen outside the Reserve[22].

This leads to charges that excluding people from wilderness is morally repugnant, ecologically incoherent, intellectually indefensible, politically dubious and ultimately simply an elitist Western construct of questionable value[23]. Or more pointedly: 'the Western concept of wilderness is a moral menace on whose altars the sustainable livelihoods of indigenous peoples are being mindlessly sacrificed in the name of conservation, ... for the recreation of alienated town dwellers.'[24] Christians will find principles to affirm on both sides of the argument and it can readily be noted that much of it turns on exactly how unspoiled, remote, or human-free such areas are and were, also how extensive and what opportunity costs are involved in their establishment. And obviously the more people access wilderness areas, then effectively the less wilderness there is, giving rise to a political dilemma. But we must note that the argument is essentially, at its core, a religious one arising out of the Romanticism discussed in the previous chapter.

Management Issues

There are other factors which should influence how we get our hands dirty with the practicalities of land stewardship.

Thanks to infestation of weeds and feral animals, management is usually needed, even in an 'undisturbed' national park. In the UK grey squirrels and mink introduced from North America wreak havoc with native species. In Australia, rabbits, foxes, and feral cats similarly affect native fauna by competition and predation. Introduced weeds from *Salvinia* in the waterways to vigorous shrubs such as *Mimosa pigra*, *Chrysanthemoides* and runaway creepers which choke trees all profoundly alter the vegetation, and thus the habitat of many native animals, in many places. Weeds now make up 16% of Australia's wild plant species[25] and cost some US $2 billion per year in the rural sector. The poisonous introduced cane toad *Bufo marinus* has steadily expanded its range from the east coast of Queensland and has now reached the Kakadu National Park, where its effect on native fauna is likely to eclipse all other human-induced change to date (of which mining is a small part). If nature conservation values and also aesthetic values are to be preserved, these invasions must be countered. Such management is costly. This is a practical issue, but not irrelevant to the principles canvassed.

Another management challenge for many national parks, especially in Australia and parts of the USA, is fire. Should control (prescribed) burning be undertaken to reduce the likelihood and intensity of wildfires? Should management attempt to emulate the burning practices of indigenous inhabitants prior to European settlement? Should wildfires be fought? If not, how is the risk to adjacent property handled? After the devastating bushfires in southeastern Australia early in 2003 a conference addressed the lessons from them. 'One theme that emerged repeatedly from all quarters is that State Governments are far more enthusiastic about creating electorally-popular National Parks than they are about funding the management of (them).' The parks 'are progressively degraded through infestations of weeds and feral animals and become increasing fire hazards' due to lack of fuel-reduction burning. 'The habitats—and perhaps even entire populations—of some threatened species were engulfed in the huge fires that spread through the parks of north-eastern Victoria'.[26]

The second issue is whether the economic benefits from development or use of part of a national park or similar area can lead to a portion of the revenue being dedicated and channeled to that management. This may be a surer source of funds than official budgets constantly under threat of emasculation in some far-off political oasis. Management is a huge issue in nature conservation, and it must be responsive to local perception of need. Any notion of stewardship without attention to land management is hollow.

In 1994, an ex-National Parks Service colleague and I undertook a project and produced a book of case studies[27] showing how complementary land use (involving mining and oil in particular) actually benefited conservation values, in some cases dramatically. Mostly this was with resource companies managing the land and doing a better job, because of better funding, than national park authorities. For instance, Barrow Island off the West Australian coast is an exemplary fauna reserve preserving a number of thriving species virtually extinct elsewhere. They coexist with oil wells, and the island is run by an oil company. A mainland example is Olympic Dam mine and treatment plant (and the town of Roxby Downs) which sit in a 280 square kilometre area of former pastoral land (grazed but otherwise unaltered) which has been destocked of sheep and cattle, allowing substantial regeneration of the natural arid zone ecosystem. Most (over 250 sq km) of the area is undisturbed by the mining and associated town. In fact it is managed like a national park but with much better weed and feral animal control. It has been described, by a senior public servant, as the best managed nature conservation reserve (or national park) in South Australia.

Christian Attitudes

It is noteworthy that the evangelical Declaration on the Care of Creation and commentary on it[28] avoid any utilitarian discourse of a kind that helps in considering vexed land use questions. (As mentioned in chapter 1, they do not mention mining or forestry except by way of listing the standpoints and presumed motivation of those who attack the Declaration. Perhaps it is an oversight, though others have found the issues too difficult to reconcile.)

So how should we use the land? It is clear from the Old Testament that grazing, agriculture and forestry were normal activities, and there are plenty of indications that pursuing them unsustainably or rapaciously was neither wise nor godly. But that was a fairly primitive society in its practices relating to the land. What about today with six billion people on the face of the Earth, heading for perhaps nine billion? The land remains the basis of their food and much of their fibre and building materials of various kinds, as discussed in the following chapter. The pressure on productive land is considerable, and could increase, though a well-supported school of thought suggests that increases in productivity such as

India's green revolution mean that approximately the present area under cultivation will serve a greater population. This controversy is discussed in chapter 6.

There are many aspects to take into account for any informed approach to the question of land use, including access to mineral resources. They are germane to how Christians understand all natural resources as part of creation stewardship in general and stewardship of the land in particular.

A utilitarian dimension to stewardship of land is basic if we are to be faithful in addressing human needs. In practical terms this will normally mean that various land uses are managed in a complementary fashion, and this must be on a sustainable basis.

Ultimately, we need to be able to understand why the people of Israel were exhorted, having enjoyed its agricultural, forest, and mineral bounty, to 'praise the Lord your God for the good land he has given you' (Dt 8:10). The following chapters attempt to shed some light on that.

3

The Fruit of the Earth

So how should we use the land productively today? The land remains the basis of our food and much of our fibre and building materials of various kinds.

It is agriculture, at increasing intensity and productivity, which enables six billion to be fed. If all of the world's inhabitants today relied on hunter-gatherer use of land, we would all be very hungry. The remarkable thing is that food production has been rising rapidly without a corresponding increase in land used for it (now about 11% of the land surface, and with no increase since 1960 despite a doubling of world population since then). Both food and fibre production have become steadily more intensive and agricultural technology today provides for more people than was considered feasible even a few decades ago. Genetic change has long been a means of enhancing the productivity of land, first by selective breeding and then by genetic modification in cells.

But how much of this increase is a step change due to application of fertilisers which cannot be repeated? Can the rate of increase continue? What scope remains for increased productivity due to genetic improvement?

The Unfolding Provision of Food

The story of how agriculture for food and also fibre production has developed is fascinating. It yields an understanding of how God has provided for dramatic increases in human populations. Of course not all among the world's inhabitants are well fed, and it is certain that a significant proportion were never well fed. That deficiency today is a major challenge for all, and notably Christians concerned with stewardship of God's creation on behalf of all its inhabitants.

Looking back at how food production (and to a lesser extent the production of fibres such as cotton, wool and timber) has impacted the landscape and ecology we see massive change. Some of it, such as desertification and land salinity, is unambiguously bad. Some of it has created the rural landscapes which many esteem so highly, but which are radically altered from pre-human condition. Some in tropical areas has produced a shifting mosaic of altered forest through slash and burn agriculture, constantly moving on. Some change was inevitable to achieve the food production required to feed people, some was the result of bad management, either driven by poverty and desperation or simply carelessness and incompetence. In the seas and oceans, it is not possible to know what changes have been wrought, except in more recent times, and that picture is not encouraging.

Due to the loss of original vegetation and its replacement with farmland, and the alteration of rangelends by grazing, we infer that there must have been an enormous loss of biodiversity in all this enterprise. In recent centuries the historical record documents many of the changes, for instance a quadrupling of farmland from 1700 to 1960,[1] displacing forest and grassland. Further back, it is confirmed to a large extent by fossil pollen. Awareness of the extent of this loss is a major driver of opinion today which opposes further changes in land use involving disturbance to the vegetative status quo. Remarkably, there has only been a 12% increase in farmland since 1960,[2] while world population has doubled and has been better fed. Significant advances in food storage (notably control of insect and fungal damage) and in transport have allowed better distribution of food.

Of course it is not only the direct biological change, but also the other effects of agriculture which can be catalogued as environmental impacts. These include both inexorable and potentially avoidable changes, from soil erosion to pesticide residues.

But on the positive side, it is relevant to note that whatever the overall picture and prognosis, productivity of land has increased remarkably, due to the application of technology in two principal areas: crop breeding and fertilisers. The selective breeding of improved crop and pasture varieties over hundreds of years, but most of all in the last half century, has had an enormous effect on the food yield from land. Secondly, and coupled with this, the industrial synthesis of ammonia as the basis for nitrogen fertilisers has done more than anything else to enable fourfold world population growth through the 20th century.[3] Without these two linked developments, starvation and ecological destruction would have been the main story.

The other four aspects of agricultural development, and particularly the 'Green Revolution' of the last fifty years, are irrigation to enable controlled water supply, pesticides to reduce crop losses, mechanisation and better management skills.[4] Irrigation is considered below in the section on Water.

Statistics on the increase in agricultural productivity are impressive. Over 1961-2001 the world population doubled but food production rose even faster, and in fact food production per head rose some 23% worldwide, and considerably more in developing countries.[5] Furthermore, the energy content per capita in this food consumed appears to have increased by a quarter in the last 40 years overall, and 38% in developing countries.[6] Of course such broad statistics can hide some very negative and tragic subsets, for instance the latter figures include virtually no increase in sub-Saharan Africa.[7] A more homogeneous subset of figures shows that in the past 40 years Australia's farm production has increased by 130%, with annual increases ranging from 1 to 3.5%.[8]

Much of the credit for the vision of the Green Revolution[9] has been given to Professor Norman Borlaug, who won a Nobel Peace

Prize in 1970 for his endeavours particularly in Mexico and then India. From being seemingly hopeless fifty years ago, India has come to be able to feed itself due to this Green Revolution. Africa could potentially do so even more readily, it has been suggested, but World Bank assistance to bring this about has been blocked by Western environmentalist pressure on the basis that it would be 'a recipe for disaster'—apparently because feeding these people properly might cause or allow population growth.[10] The evidence, of course, is contrary. It must be said however that the political situation in most of Africa would be unlikely to allow development to proceed as it did in India.

Fertiliser use is the first and most contentious pillar of twentieth century agricultural development. In Europe after 1920, North America after 1930 and Japan after 1960 fertiliser use, along with the advent of irrigation, enabled productivity to increase without expansion of cropland.[11] Since 1950 in developing countries, fertiliser use has increased almost nine-fold.[12] This has brought about a major improvement in food production, and without it very much more good land would need to be under cultivation. But is has been essentially a step change, and over much of the world further increases in fertiliser application are unlikely to be beneficial.[13] Africa is the main part of the world where there is still major scope for agricultural improvement due to fertilisers.

Fertilisers have not only an economic but also an energy/hydrocarbon cost, nitrogen fertilisers depending generally on natural gas as a raw material. This is abundant now, but set to become more expensive, which will raise the cost of continuing inputs which are likely to be necessary to maintain present production.

The second major part the story of agricultural development, and particularly the Green Revolution, centres on new crop varieties, especially corn, wheat and rice. These are adapted through selective breeding to be much more productive in the particular places they are grown.[14] For instance, some may germinate earlier (thus have longer growing season), grow faster (maybe allowing more crops per year, or avoiding summer dry spells), have shorter stems (hence allocating more nutrients into the grain and more efficient harvesting), be disease-resistant (reducing pesticide requirement, or simply increasing the harvest) or drought-resistant (allowing a more extensive range—notably corn). In many cases varieties combine several of these characteristics. High-yield strains accounted for 95% of China's rice and maize by 1990,[15] and new wheat varieties now make up some 90% of the production in developing countries.[16] They have also transformed agricultural productivity in the UK, where wheat for bread-making previously had to imported.[17] Increased yields in UK also mean that less land is now required for cultivation.

Selective breeding was the main factor in a twofold improvement in livestock productivity over the last fifty years.[18] There would be many examples, but one of note is the change in beef cattle across northern Australia, a subtropical environment. The cattle industry had depended on European breeds for many years, which were unsuited to this environment. But the introduction of southeast Asian Brahman genetic types[19] and the consequent development of several new registered breeds has changed the scene. Beef cattle with these bloodlines are now less stressed by heat, more resistant to external parasites (notably ticks), get significantly more nitrogen out of tropical pastures and can forage better in shrubs and trees, so give about 30% greater productivity.[20] This example is typical in that it shows a directed adaptation of breeds to their environment.

A similar example is a current project with Thai native cattle in their own environment. Bulls from a national herd are being improved by scientifically-directed selective breeding and then supplied to village herds, potentially resulting in huge, sustainable increases in beef productivity while utilising low-quality feed and limited management capabilities of traditional farm units.[21]

Since 1950 pesticides have also become a major input to agriculture. In 1960 insects consumed or spoiled almost one third of Asia's rice crop,[22] so there was obviously considerable need for them even before the other measures took effect. Both fertilisers and pesticides add considerably to the working capital needs of farmers, which underlines the need for institutional arrangements to accompany such developments (see later section).

The increased fertiliser and pesticide use has had some significant environmental consequences, in eutrophication of waterways

---

Food Production in Genesis:

Food production is the earliest divine provision or human activity which raises questions of interaction with the God-created aspects of the environment and which threatens biodiversity. In Genesis 1:29 God says 'I give you every seed-bearing plant on the face of the whole earth and every tree that has fruit with seed in it. They will be yours for food.' In Genesis 2:9 we have the garden 'with all kinds of trees ....good for food'. The man was turned loose here 'to work it and take care of it', the working apparently being with a view to food production. After the fall (Gen 3:17-19) man continues to be focused on the soil and plants for food, though food production becomes fraught.

Cain and Abel in Genesis 4 are farmer and herdsman respectively, though as judgement on his fratricide Cain becomes a nomad. We don't know much about the third brother Seth, or how his successors were fed through to the time of Noah. After the flood we have God's promise that 'As long as the earth endures, seedtime and harvest ..... will never cease' (Gen 8:22), implying an agricultural economy at that time, and indeed we later find that Noah was 'a man of the soil' who included a vineyard in his endeavours (Gen 9:20). In blessing Noah and his sons, God says to them (Gen 9:3) 'Everything that lives and moves will be food for you. Just as I gave you the green plants, I now give you everything.' He then reiterates the early commission: 'Be fruitful and increase in number; multiply on the earth and increase upon it' (Gen 9:7).

---

due to fertiliser run-off, and pollution from pesticide run-off. The former gives rise to algal proliferation ('blooms') and leads to depletion of oxygen in the water, thus severely depleting animal life there. These are clear negatives, but in many parts of the world they are accepted as the price of more food, while efforts continue to minimise them. In fact these effects are not confined to artificial fertilisers. More than half of England's farmland is subject to severe restrictions on spreading manure, due to water pollution from its run-off.

Another negative effect of pesticides is chemical residues in meat (e.g., due to feeding cotton meal to stock). Dipping cattle to control ticks has been virtually eliminated with introduction of Brahman (tick-resistant) genetics, which removes that means of contamination. Sheep strains genetically more resistant to internal worm burdens are being developed, thus reducing (but not eliminating) drenching requirements.[23]

Mechanisation brought about huge gains in productivity, and also environmental changes due to the need for extensive cultivation on large fields—eliminating many hedgerows for example, and monocultures.

As well as the technological innovations, scientifically-based management practices have been a factor in increased productivity from the land. One of these is integrated pest management, a rediscovery and development of traditional ecological methods of pest control by ensuring that there are sufficient predators (typically both insect and bird to control insect pests, for example). The rediscovery of this has been partly due to misuse of insecticides in the last few decades, and is thus a pointer to the virtues of more ecological and less technocratic solutions associated with stewardship of creation.

However, this is not to say that organic farming (without added synthetic fertilisers or pesticides) is the way forward. Plants take up minerals and nutrients in essentially inorganic forms, and so there is no special virtue in fertilising with compost instead of something out of a bag from a factory (though the soil structure may be much helped by the former). Certainly there is huge scope for using legumes to fix nitrogen into the soil, for crop rotation which improves soil condition, and there are many other techniques now broadly called 'organic' which should be employed, but total reliance on them would be devastating to world agricultural productivity.[24]

Since 1960, in developing countries, rice, corn and wheat production per hectare has increased hugely.[25] These increases are due to all the factors involved in the Green Revolution together. Today, it is estimated that 40% of all crop nitrogen is from synthetic fertiliser, and about one third of human protein consumption is from synthetic fertiliser[26]—hence ultimately from fossil hydrocarbons.

Food is not simply from the land however, and no treatment with biblical pretensions should omit fishing. Ocean fisheries have fed many people for millennia. But here the development of technology, both boats and electronic equipment to find the fish, has resulted in overfishing, leading to a major degradation of world fisheries, especially in the last two decades. In the 1980s the last new fisheries were opened up, and total catches from the oceans have not increased since.[27]

A large part of the problem is that oceans are part of the global commons, not the responsibility of any particular country, so that the cost of restraint by an individual is usually much greater than the benefit—the long-term recovery of fish stocks is more likely to benefit others. Even where national ownership of waters is claimed, there is a major problem in policing the areas concerned—the oceans are something of an international free-for-all. Another part of the problem close to shore is pollution, especially from farming. The solutions are clear enough, but hard to implement in international waters. Meanwhile, the supply of fish from aquaculture is rising strongly and by 1996 was approaching one third of that from ocean fishing.[28] If this trend continues we have a marine equivalent of the transition on land from hunter to farmer.

Considering the whole food situation, there are still a lot of people without enough to eat, so the job is far from complete, but the limitations are human. We are a long way from being able to point to any lack of provision on God's part. What has been achieved in the last half century is remarkable, and testimony to God's provision in a variety of ways, including through chemical and biological technologies.

Provision for Forest Products and Minerals

In forestry, management practices have given some productivity gains and in plantation timbers selective breeding is giving more. But in contrast to agriculture, the area logged each year has risen inexorably as the appetite of modern civilisation for paper products from wood fibre compounds the demand for structural timber.[29] This increased logging has been almost entirely in developing countries, and there are serious questions about the sustainability of it, especially on poor soils. Forestry as such needs to be distinguished from logging which is deliberate land clearance for agriculture (i.e., land use change) in areas such as the Amazon basin. Here Brazil has 360 million hectares of forest with potential for timber production, and in some states this is being inexorably lost. For 2004 the Brazilian government's own statistics showed a loss of 2.35 million hectares of forest, capping off two decades of losses of 1.5 to 2 million hectares per year. There is said to be more abandoned cattle pasture from clearing in the 1970s and 1980s than there is active cattle pasture, the soil nutrients having been depleted.[30]

Much forestry (for sound scientific/ecological reasons, mimicking the natural wildfire regime) involves clear-felling areas, then burning the slash (remnant trimmings etc.). Though the areas of such logging coupes should be limited for aesthetic and biodiversity reasons to 10-20 hectares at a time, and in total comprise less than half of the overall area,[31] clear-felling is most unattractive aesthetically. Many photos attest to the presumed 'rape of the land' in such forestry, but those publishing them pejoratively fail to reveal how the same areas look a decade or two later with vigorous regrowth!

Statistics about loss of forest cover worldwide are difficult to interpret, since often they do not have any qualitative dimension. Where forests are cleared for permanent agriculture the picture is reasonably clear, but elsewhere it is not. Official figures showing very little loss in forest cover over the last fifty years[32] may be inaccurate or at best they may obscure a greater loss of biomass and biodiversity. Much anecdotal evidence suggests that tropical rainforests are not being managed sustainably—the figure of 10 million hectares lost per year is credible but probably overstated.[33] Tropical deforestation is said to account for up to seven billion tonnes of carbon dioxide emissions per year—not much less than that from power generation.[34]

It may well be that, in line with the historic transition from the hunter-gatherer economy to intensive agriculture, forestry progressively makes the transition from logging native forests (with regeneration) to plantation forestry which has no regard for biodiversity or what species are native to the particular land involved.[35] That shift is already well advanced in developed countries, but much of their timber and paper fibre currently comes from less-developed countries or less-developed regions.

While forests of some kind cover about one third of the world's land surface, only 3-5% of this is plantation.[36] However it is the plantation area which in many parts of the world provides much of the wood and wood fibre,[37] and that portion is growing due largely to economic considerations. For instance, natural tropical forest has a low yield—1-2 m³/ha/yr, whereas plantations yield 30-40 m³/ha/yr, so that natural tropical forestry is simply not competitive with plantation forestry on a sustainable basis.[38] As noted, it is this plantation portion also which is most amenable to genetic improvement through selective breeding. But there is a major cost in diminished biodiversity, just as there is in intensive agriculture.

Looking beneath the land surface, how should we view the world's mineral resources? They are clearly part of what is entrusted to us for use. For instance the Exodus Israelites were promised a 'good land' where the food will be plentiful and 'where the rocks are iron and you can dig copper out of the hills' (as they proceeded to do)—as part of God's abundant provision for them (Deut 8:9). Today our civilisation, not to mention the survival of most of the world's population, clearly depends on them. So why is their extraction regarded as a slightly dubious activity?

Many may be unaware that while some mining results in the total destruction of a limited area of land, such mining is normally conditional upon its full biological rehabilitation afterwards. Western governments (at least) typically hold a bond sufficient to ensure rehabilitation should the company fail along the way.[39] Of course other mining involves little disturbance.[40] Zero release of pollutants from a mine site is now the norm. These measures, it must be acknowledged, are in response to some major environmental impacts from mining in several parts of the world up until the 1970s, and in a few cases, the 1990s.

Should credible rehabilitation plans be a condition for allowing any short-term land use such as mining? Is it ever acceptable to leave mined land desolate? Is land use change for the longer term acceptable in principle?

These are issues handled differently in various parts of the world, but from a Christian stewardship perspective some rigorous standards are desirable, if they are affordable by the beneficiaries of any mining. From a company's point of view in a globalised industry, consistent standards are essential for its credibility and reputation, whether required locally or not. The dilemma then is that if these are too costly to justify an international company commencing a mine in the first place, local people may miss out on its benefits—though they might be happy to bear some environmental cost. In which direction does Christian stewardship default then—to the needs of local people despite some environmental costs, or to strict environmental standards? (There will also be other complications, plus conflicting motivations, so that each such situation is very complex!)[41]

Minerals and energy are discussed further in chapters 4 and 5.

While sustainable agriculture and forestry may be superficially more compatible with the garden model of creation stewardship than mining, we need to remember that growing a crop of any kind usually involves first denuding the land then sowing the seed, all this being on land which may have had its original ecosystem totally destroyed in historical times.

Water for Life

Like clean air, fresh water tends to be taken for granted when it available and accepted as a severely limiting factor where it is not. As well as needs for domestic use, irrigation has been a conspicuous feature of agriculture for thousands of years. Irrigation projects have sought to make fresh water available where nature denied it, and there have been both beneficial and adverse effects from this. Land area irrigated rose fivefold during the 20th century and in 1990 irrigated land comprised 16% of the world's cultivated area, accounting for 30% of food production. But half of the diverted and dammed water was wasted by evaporation or infiltration before being used. Balancing the benefits, there were some spectacular ecological and economic disasters in it all. In fact some schemes damming or diverting surface waters rank with the greatest environmental impacts of the century. In the 1990s, salinity seriously affected ten percent of the irrigated land and the problem was increasing. Also some irrigation has tapped groundwater at unsustainable levels, effectively mining it and seriously depleting aquifers in the USA, Libya and Saudi Arabia.[42]

Urban demands for water have steadily increased and in some cases take a large share of what is available. Overall, water use per capita has more than doubled over the last century, and today almost two thirds is used in irrigation, a quarter for industry, and the balance domestically.[43]

At the dawn of this century it is noteworthy that potable water is seen as increasingly problematical in many places, and therefore needs to be a focus of concern and further action. Already much water is recycled after use in cities—it is said that a glass of water from the tap in Rotterdam, near the mouth of the Rhine River, has been drunk five times already! Elsewhere recycling is only for agricultural use, if that. There is scope for doing much more.

In Melbourne, a city of three million people in a dry continent, sewage has been pumped to an area of fertile soil in a rain shadow nearby and used to irrigate pasture which raises excellent beef. This far-sighted scheme began in the late 1800s. But in the same city until recently it was illegal to catch rainwater for domestic use off roofs! And beyond this single (and sometimes smelly) irrigation scheme, the balance of sewage with all its nutrients goes straight into the sea (after treatment), a huge waste.

Stewardship of fresh water needs to consider the use of nutrients in waste water and the recycling of much more than now, after appropriate treatment. An estimated one fifth of the world's population does not have access to safe drinking water, and this is a major cause of ill health. The proportion is likely to increase due to population growth relative to water resources. The worst-affected areas are the arid and semiarid regions of Asia and North Africa. Wars over access to water, not simply energy and mineral resources, are conceivable.

Finally, there will need to be increasing attention to desalination to provide potable water. Most desalination today uses fossil fuels, and thus contributes to increased levels of greenhouse gases. Total world capacity is approaching 30 million cubic metres per day of potable water, in over 10,000 plants. Half of these are in the Middle East. The major technologies in use are the multi-stage flash (MSF) distillation process using steam, and reverse osmosis (RO) driven by electric pumps. Desalination is an energy-intensive process

THE FRUIT OF THE EARTH

which can use a variety of low-temperature heat sources, including solar energy, or electricity. Nuclear power has been recognised[44] as an obvious non-greenhouse source for both heat and electricity.

Manipulating Genetics[45]

The Green Revolution of the last forty years depended substantially on selective breeding of crop and livestock varieties. Taking this one step further, and accelerating it, is genetic manipulation or modification (GM)[46] by molecular biology techniques. The results are broadly the same, and the technology is part of a continuum. Many effects achieved by genetic alteration in the laboratory can be gained, albeit more slowly, by selective breeding. With better understanding of plant genetics, selective breeding is now not much slower than GM, but GM is able to draw on a much wider source of genetic material than what can be interbred. The agricultural focus has been on pest and disease resistance of crops, and herbicide tolerance.

GM technology was developed in the 1970s and has been widely applied in medical and agricultural areas—the latter to produce novel transgenic crop varieties of cotton, oilseed rape (Canola), soy, tobacco, potato and maize. In 2003 the estimated area of transgenic crops was 68 million hectares (more than three times the area of the UK) in 13 countries, with the proportion of that area in developing countries increasing (24% in 2000).[47]

A number of specific traits are sought in GM crops:[48] virus resistance, insect tolerance, herbicide tolerance, as well as the traditional attributes of improved yield, growth characteristics, cold, salinity and drought tolerance, and nutritional quality (e.g., Golden Rice) or other food characteristics such as increased shelf life.

Virus resistance enables crops such as rice in Africa to thrive and avoid other diseases. Insect-tolerant crops (due to intrinsic insecticides), notably cotton (for bollworms) require much less insecticide to produce an acceptable product and yield. In India, yields of GM cotton have been 80% higher than with non-GM varieties[49] and in China about 65% of the cotton grown is GM, giving a significant increase in yield. A spin-off from this is that Chinese companies provide strong competition to Monsanto in world markets. China has also developed GM strains of rice which are insect and disease-resistant.[50] A current challenge is to develop a GM cassava which is resistant to viral attack.

Herbicide-tolerant crops enable chemical weed control (e.g., with broad spectrum glyphosate) and thus minimise soil disturbance,[51] giving a clear economic benefit and, by most accounts, also an ecological one. They have been grown commercially in the USA since 1995, 85% of Canadian oilseed rape is transgenic, and applications are pending for GM Canola in Australia.[52]

Golden Rice incorporates three genes (two from daffodils, one from a micro-organism) to enhance vitamin A levels and counter blindness in children. This has profound relevance to the health of one third of the world's population, especially since the variety is not patented or restricted in its availability to all. Hundreds of millions in Africa and Asia suffer from vitamin A deficiency and many children lose their sight from it. A mere 100 grams of Golden Rice would provide half of a person's daily need, but its use is blocked by anti-GM campaigning and ensuing regulation.

Four countries grew 99% of the GM crops in 2000: USA, Canada, Argentina and China. The dominant GM crop in 2000 was soybean (58% of area) followed by maize, cotton and Canola. In the USA, three quarters of the cotton is now transgenic, and much the same is true in Australia, where it has been grown since 1996. For all crops, herbicide tolerance is the main trait to be engineered (74% of area in 2000), followed by insect resistance (19%) or both (7%).

About one third of medicines used today are derived from plants, and GM techniques have considerable potential to make such pharmaceuticals more readily available. Already GM techniques enable production in plants of components of vaccines, reducing the use of animals in this role.

With conventional techniques, plants or animals with particular characteristics are selected and used for breeding. Much the same happens with GM techniques, except that the net can be cast wider, well beyond the species, and the selection of traits can be more specific (so that unwanted genes are not also introduced).[53] For example, researchers have inserted a bacterial gene into maize (Bt

76

maize) to give it resistance to particular insect pests, and similarly with Bt cotton making it unpalatable to bollworms. It is interesting that some 1000 tonnes less insecticide was used on cotton in the USA in 1999, compared with 1998, as GM varieties expanded. In China, there has been an 80% reduction in pesticide use due to planting of Bt cotton.[54]

The similarity between GM techniques and conventional ones is evident in the fact that short-stalked wheat has been derived both ways, as has herbicide-resistant Canola. In the former case, the GM technique has enabled the gene to be transferred to rice, without the problem of bringing with it unwanted characteristics.[55] The short stem characteristic gives a stronger, shorter plant which can respond better to fertilisers, and puts more of its biomass into the grain.[56]

The benefits of GM crops are the same as those for selective breeding: more food or fibre grown over a wider range of conditions at lower cost, and sometimes a better product. However, GM is expensive to develop[57] and thus has so far been largely directed to where a commercial return is most likely. As techniques are refined and the GM becomes better accepted, government can be expected to invest so as to bring GM to a wider market, including applications which are principally of benefit to poorer people in subsistence agriculture. This is already evident in China.

There are concerns that GM genes could escape to wild plants or other crops, with adverse consequences environmentally or for the agricultural system itself. These possibilities are being addressed, but on the whole the risk is no greater than for conventionally-bred varieties and nor is it clear that increased biodiversity brought about thus is necessarily bad. Another concern is for pests developing resistance to insect-tolerant crops, and again this is simply a more acute version of the same problem with selectively-bred crops. Ethical concerns centre on failure to respect the distinctions of species, and interfering with nature.

GM foods have been the most contentious aspect of the technology.[58] They may be any of several different things: foods which incorporate intact GM material (e.g., Golden Rice, long shelf-life tomatoes), foods which incorporate broken up GM material (e.g., flour from soy, wheat or maize), or foods which do not incorporate any GM material but which are from plants whose growth was enhanced due to GM (e.g., oil from GM Canola, sugar from GM beet).

In the UK the Royal Society concluded that GM was an important means to 'increase the production of main food staples, improve the efficiency of production, reduce the environmental impact of agriculture, and provide access to food for small-scale farmers'.[59] In 2001 the UK Evangelical Alliance Policy Commission on GM Crops & Foods produced a carefully-hedged and qualified set of conclusions in support of the technology. While favouring the development and introduction of GM crops, they pointed to the need 'for a moral basis for technologies which can promote and sustain the global production of food, rooted in the principles of sound ecology, economics and social justice.'[60]

Late in 2002, the President of the Royal Society, Lord May, said that while environmental questions should be at the heart of the national debate on GM crops, they should centre on appropriate uses rather than visceral rejection of the technology itself. He said that green activists opposing biotechnology tended to ignore the much greater ecological problems caused by natural plant species which were invasive.[61] He criticised those who 'know by dogma, instinct or political ideology that GM crops are bad, and the scientific facts are irrelevant,' and the pressure groups which 'continue to propagate worries about the safety of GM foods, despite the weight of evidence to the contrary.'

In October 2003 the results of UK farm-scale evaluations of GM herbicide-resistant crops showed that two out of the three—oilseed rape and sugar beet—showed an adverse impact on biodiversity (of weeds), but this was from the herbicides used, not the plants themselves. In other words it reflected better weed control in the intensive agriculture regime rather than GM as such. Better weed control leading to increased yields is precisely why the strains have been developed! Much non-GM Canola grown (60% in Australia) is already resistant to one major herbicide due to selective breeding.

In mid 2003 the Vatican declared that GM foods were vital to addressing world starvation and malnutrition, thereby taking sides rather pointedly against the EU position—and more broadly against the neo-romanticism discussed in chapter 1.[62]

In mid 2004 the US National Academy of Sciences issued a report[63] making it clear that genetically-modified crops posed no greater health hazard than those developed by selective breeding. Safety evaluation must be based on the foods themselves, not on the method used to create them. The report was sponsored by relevant US federal agencies.

The strong ideological opposition to GM foods, centred in Europe, has not extended to GM medical products or pharmaceuticals, nor to GM fibres such as cotton (where GM is becoming almost ubiquitous). In this regard the campaign is similar to that against nuclear power, where the same basic technology applied for medical purposes is widely accepted, along with plutonium-derived smoke detectors in almost every home.[64] But behind both are reservations about how we apply science, and fear of unfamiliar risks even if they are demonstrably small.

We have an ethical obligation to explore the benefits and possible hazards of GM food for the variety of reasons mentioned above. My own view is of strong support for GM technology as part of God's provision in line with technology generally, to enable effective human stewardship of his creation, serving the needs of people on a sustainable basis—especially in relation to food. The qualifications and caveats enunciated by the Evangelical Alliance are essentially those I would apply to any use of technology.[65] I think Christians need to stand firm against the Romanticism (and sometimes neo-pagan pseudoscience or simply junk science) which opposes GM technology outright.

Human Institutions

The preceding sections have outlined much good news—good that God has endowed us with so much, and good that human science and technology have enabled so great an expansion in productivity that exceeds even the increase in population which depends on it.

But any reading of a newspaper or acquaintance with parts of the world outside of Western affluence reminds us that all is not well and that hundreds of millions live in poverty, subject to malnutrition and ill health.[66] There is no room for complacency. These problems are certainly very relevant to our stewardship of God's creation. This short section will attempt to flag some issues, but not expound them.

The need for wealth creation, however rudimentary, to lift individuals and communities out of mere subsistence has been mentioned. With more and more people needing food but living remote from where food is produced, the need for markets scarcely needs emphasis. Markets presuppose some social and political stability, however, and that is lacking in many places.

But apart from political instability, military intervention and corruption, which need no extended comment here, are other questions. How free should markets be, how regulated, what institutional arrangements pertain for property rights, employment, enforcement of contracts, legally-secure investment, affordable borrowing, taxation, accessible justice and so on? In the West we take functional forms of all these for granted, and in return for taxes expect non-corrupt bureaucracy, independent judiciary and sound economic management by government as well as practical provision such as transport, water, electricity and other infrastructure. Elsewhere, the lack of proper institutional provision for any one of these basic requirements can mean that the most productive potential in any part of the world is severely limited, while people remain in great need.

The whole way of treating land is fundamental to enabling the developing world to join the rest. If any doubt about the importance of property rights—especially for land—remains, the former Soviet Union is a recent case study. But property rights involve effective and transferable title which is legally secure as well as an infrastructure of surveyors, non-corrupt public servants, banks, lawyers, etc. If land and resource ownership is unclear, development will be minimal and probably inadequate to meet needs.[67] It is relevant to note here that capitalism in a moral, political, and institutional vacuum will never make sense—we need to address it (or any alternative) in the context of democracy, freedom of speech and related liberties, and of property rights, as well as enforcement of contracts, justice and other infrastructural provision. Capitalism cannot sensibly be considered apart from its multifarious context, and much of the critique of it would be more profitably directed at elements of that context in particular cases.

Corresponding with these problems in developing countries are obscene agricultural subsidies[68] in some developed countries, totalling hundreds of billions of US dollars or Euros per year[69] to keep farm products from the developing world out of their markets and leading to waste on a grand scale. A UK *Times* leader called the €40 billion per year Common Agricultural Policy (CAP) 'perhaps the least ethical and the most inefficient example of public policy to be found in the civilised world. It ensures plenty and surplus at a high price in this continent while imposing poverty and starvation, at a much higher price, on much of the Third World. ... It has absolutely no redeeming features' (except, one assumes, to some regional politicians).[70] Each European cow is subsidised about US$1 per day (other reports have twice this figure)—more than the poorest one fifth of the world's humans have to live on. As the UK's Catholic Agency for Overseas Development put it: 'It is better to be a cow in Europe than a human being in the South.'[71] The chief direct effect of agricultural subsidies is the dumping of surplus subsidised produce in developing countries so as to destabilise markets, provide a disincentive to food production and neutralise wealth creation there.[72] Tariff protection imposed by developed countries on imports of food and fibre from developing countries is a further disincentive to rational use of resources and wealth creation where it is most needed.[73]

Today in many developing countries there is a level of government indebtedness which chronically saps the ability to address many of these issues, notably provision of functional infrastructure such as water,[74] electricity, sanitation, roads, transport and telecommunications.

A corollary of pointing out the importance of institutional supports for food production and economic activity generally is to note their fragility and vulnerability. It is the essence of civilisation to harness human endeavour and advance from subsistence, but tragically we often see how easy it is through warfare, terrorism or tyranny to retreat again.

Globalisation involving the liberalisation of markets and the removal of barriers to trade and investment has caused unprecedented growth in many countries—those which opened their economies, through the 1990s.[75] Poverty was markedly reduced. But globalisation is meaningless to those who are unable to function in their economy because of basic deficiencies in the areas mentioned above—or if it means anything it is negative. But Christians can have a vision of the global economy where the deficiencies are worked on constantly, where justice is constantly improved, where opportunities expand (especially for the poorest) and where exploitation in the pejorative sense of that term is curbed. The difficulties in implementing that vision do not negate it, and therefore should not overwhelm those committed to bringing it about.

Unfortunately much Christian comment on the issue is prejudiced and unhelpful—imputing unworthy motives to some parties, and implying that our own worthy sentiments and motives should thereby prevail regardless of the practical questions above. Others take the view that markets with free trade and movement of capital are all that is required, without stopping to look at the poverty traps and dysfunctional structures which hinder people, or without acknowledging that companies and other institutions cannot be expected to transcend the moral character of the people who run them.

The point here is that Christian stewardship of God's creation must inevitably serve people, and hence must grapple with these messy, challenging, and sometimes quite perverse social, economic and political issues of our day, however depressing and intractable they may be.

4

Mineral and Energy Resources

The conventional wisdom that growing human populations, increasing pollution and diminishing resources threaten the future of humanity[1] needs challenging on several grounds. First, like food, resource availability has more than kept pace with population increase, though we need a wider understanding of how this is so. Secondly, there is the distinct prospect of world population growth slowing down, as it has in the developed world. Thirdly, there is at least as much good news as bad on the pollution front.

Perhaps the best illustration of the effective sustainability of resource use is provided by an anecdote. In 1980 two eminent men, fierce critics of one another, made a bet regarding the real market price of five metal commodities over the next decade. They agreed that this would provide a reliable indicator of the abundance of those metals. Paul Ehrlich, an ecologist, bet that because the world was exceeding its carrying capacity, food and commodities would start to run out in the 1980s and prices in real terms would therefore rise. Julian Simon, an economist, said that resources were effectively so abundant that prices would fall in real terms. He invited Ehrlich to nominate which commodities would be used to test the matter, and they settled on these. In 1990 Ehrlich paid up —all the prices had fallen.[2]

There are certainly some major questions about how we use resources, and also on several fronts we need to lift our game in environmental stewardship. But the world's resources are unbelievably abundant. Where any is limited, substitutes are usually found. Globally, as will be argued here, there is no prospect of us running out of any natural resource that we actually need in the foreseeable future, given a modicum of care, common sense and adaptability. God's provision is vastly greater than generally understood or accepted, and if we can flesh out our understanding of that in practical terms it allows a robust rather than a timid approach to the question of sustainability.

Where are the Limits to Growth?

The notion of finite resources has captured a major place in conventional wisdom. In the last few decades it flourished as a result of a very influential study from the Club of Rome, a distinguished group of academics, published in 1972 titled *The Limits to Growth*.[3] This was subsequently critiqued vigorously and has been somewhat discredited by the passage of time (as are many lesser forecasts!), but its influence lingers and it has had profound effects on our present resource situation as described below.

Of course it is not so much the concept of limits which is flawed, as the assumptions which go with it. As noted in passing in an earlier chapter, humankind has bumped up against limits since the dawn of time, but has responded in the kinds of ways described in the following sections. We need to challenge the assumptions about limits, while not being dismissive of the concerns or denying the truism of limits. The question is, where are the limits? and if we are in any danger of running up against some of them, as perhaps today with global warming, how do we deal with the situation constructively? The alarmist utterances of some high-profile environmental prophets such as Paul Ehrlich have been exposed as nonsense both by time and argument.

The successor to Limits to Growth as a doomsday bogey is the more subtle misapplication of the principle of Sustainable Development. It is sometimes stated that because a particular mineral resource is non-renewable, therefore its ongoing use (unless with 100% recycle) is incompatible with Sustainable Development (SD) principles. It is certainly sometimes said of uranium and fossil fuels that their use is 'unsustainable' on a resource basis. There are three lines of response: first, SD is sustainable *Development*, which envisages such use to meet present needs in a qualified way, and ceasing all such use would plainly bring life to a halt for many. Secondly, if such non-renewable resources were never to be used they would cease to be resources in any meaningful sense, and logically this means even for future generations. Thirdly, the present use of a particular resource sets in train an economic dynamic which both regulates the rate of use by price mechanisms and ensures substitution as or when abundance declines, so that it will never run out in any absolute sense. This dynamic relationship is illustrated in Figure 1, which I drafted when developing an understanding of these issues from within a major mining company in the 1980s.

Figure 1.

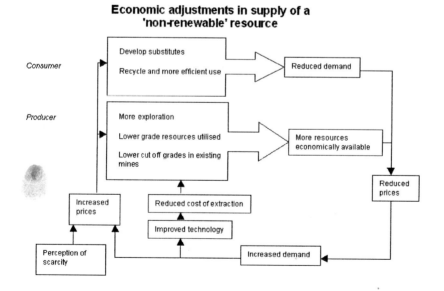

Economic adjustments in supply of a 'non-renewable' resource

This could be extended to a fourth point which is that the use of some non-renewable resources is absolutely necessary to create access to others, as well as to renewable sources such as solar and wind—both being very resource-intensive in all but fuel. An additional consideration relevant to this question is that of opportunity cost, which should drive us to meet needs with those suitable resources which have no other likely use (contrasting for instance uranium and natural gas).

Creating or Developing New Resources through Technology

It is meaningless to speak of a resource of any particular material until someone has thought of a way to use it. In this sense, human ingenuity quite literally creates new resources, historically, currently and prospectively. That is the most fundamental level at which technology creates resources, by making particular minerals useable in new ways. Often these then substitute to some degree for others which are becoming scarcer, as indicated by rising prices.

More particularly, if a known mineral deposit cannot be mined, processed and marketed economically, it does not constitute a resource in any practical sense. Many factors other than price determine whether a particular mineral deposit can be considered a useable resource—the scale of mining and processing, the technology brought to bear, its location in relation to markets, and so on. The application of human ingenuity, through technology, alters the significance of all these factors, and is thus a second means of 'creating' resources—allowing an unfolding or unpacking of God's creation which is economically feasible. In effect, portions of the Earth's crust are reclassified as resources.

An excellent example of this application of technology to create resources is in the Pilbara region of Western Australia. Until the 1960s the vast iron ore deposits there were simply geological curiosities, despite their very high grade. Australia had been perceived as short of iron ore. With modern large-scale mining technology and the advent of heavy duty railways and bulk shipping which could economically get the iron ore from the mine (well inland) through the ports of Dampier and Port Hedland to Japan, these became one of the nation's main mineral resources. For the last 35 years Hamersley Iron (Rio Tinto), Mount Newman (BHP-Billiton) and others have been at the forefront of Australia's mineral exporters, drawing upon these 'new' orebodies. This both creates much wealth for all Australians and supplies the needs of many people in other parts of the world.[4]

Just over a hundred years ago aluminium was a precious metal, not because it was scarce, but because it was almost impossible to reduce the oxide to the metal, which was therefore fantastically expensive. In 1855 a bar of aluminium was a feature at the Paris Exhibition. With the discovery of the Hall-Heroult process in 1886, the cost of producing aluminium plummeted to about one twentieth of what it had been and that metal has steadily become more commonplace. It now competes with iron in many applications, and copper in others, as well as having its own widespread uses in every aspect of our lives. Some 25 million tonnes of it are produced each year,[5] with another 8 million tonnes recovered from scrap. Not only was a virtually new material provided for people's use by this technological breakthrough, but enormous quantities of bauxite worldwide progressively became a valuable resource. Without the technological breakthrough, these deposits would have remained simply geological features akin to laterites.

The development of new technologies which are able to utilise otherwise non-useable or uneconomic iron ore 'fines' and other low grade materials which otherwise aren't quite in the category of commercial-grade ore is another good example of creating resources, by enabling potentially discarded materials to be reclassified as resources.[6] It is in a way a subset of the broad thrust to utilise all wastes for some positive good. Incremental improvements in processing technology at all plants are less obvious but nevertheless very significant also in creating or at least extending resources. Over many years they are probably as important as the historic technological breakthroughs.

Improved energy efficiency in metal smelters has resulted in large savings of energy and this is another very important aspect of making resources go further.

At the level of manufacturing, research into making more drink cans from each kilogram of aluminium or more widgets from every tonne of iron, etc., are means of stretching resources and making what we have go further through more efficient use.[7] Recycling of aluminium, lead and other metals is another aspect of this, principally in respect of energy efficiency.

To achieve meaningful sustainability, the combined effects of mineral exploration and the development of technology need to be creating resources at least as fast as they are being used. There is no question that in respect to metals this is generally so, though for oil and gas any sustainability needs to be achieved as much by substitution. For metals, recycling also helps.

One significant development over human history can be noted, which is relevant to the accumulation of carbon dioxide in the atmosphere. That is the succession of fuels which have provided energy for the world. Initially firewood was pre-eminent, and it still is in some parts of the world. But the industrial revolution was enabled by coal, then oil became the lifeblood of industry and transport, this being partly displaced by natural gas from the 1970s. The points to note are the increasing sophistication of the infrastructure required to deliver these fuels over long distances, and the decreasing carbon content of them. It is tempting to look forward to further reductions in carbon intensity of fuels as hydrogen comes into widespread use, accompanied by a further increase in technological sophistication for its production and storage.[8]

Economics Determining Resources

Whether a particular mineral deposit is sensibly available as a resource will also depend on the market price of the mineral concerned. If it costs more to get it out of the ground than its value warrants, it can hardly be classified as a resource (unless there is market distortion due to government subsidies of some kind). Therefore, the resources available will depend on the market price, which in turn depends on world demand for the particular mineral and the costs of supplying that demand. The dynamic equilibrium between supply and demand also gives rise to substitution of other materials when scarcity looms (or the price is artificially elevated). This then is the third aspect of creating resources.[9]

The best known example of the interaction of markets with resource availability is in the oil industry. The Club of Rome in 1972 said that total world oil reserves amounted to 550 billion barrels, yet over the next 20 years 600 billion barrels were consumed and reserves in 1990 stood at 900 billion barrels.[10] The response in the early 1970s by OPEC to the Club of Rome and *Limits to Growth* thinking was for it to suddenly increase the price of oil fourfold, which was understandable. However, this action caused several things to happen at both producer and consumer levels.

The producers, and particularly Western oil companies, dramatically increased their exploration effort, and applied ways to boost oil recovery from previously 'exhausted' or uneconomic wells. At the consumer end, increased prices meant massive substitution of other fuels and greatly increased capital expenditure in more efficient plant and motor vehicles. As a result of the former activities, oil resources increased dramatically. As a result of the latter, oil use fell slightly to 1975 and in the longer perspective did not increase globally from 1973 to 1986. Forecasts in 1972, which had generally predicted a doubling of oil consumption in ten years, proved quite wrong.

Oil is in fact a well-known example of a major resource whose production is evidently approaching its peak and will decline, requiring more of the substitutes which have already been brought forward. The geologist M. King Hubbert predicted in 1956 that US production would peak soon after 1970 and then decline. It did, and world production seems set to follow suit perhaps as early as 2005[11]. Much of the substitution for oil has been by natural gas, and recently (due to both economics and greenhouse concerns) gas has been applied to the traditional roles of coal in such uses as large-scale electricity generation. The wisdom of this will be tested in the next decade, but it already looks very suspect as prices have unsurprisingly risen. Certainly oil will never run out in any absolute sense—it will simply become too expensive to use as liberally as we now do.

Another example is again provided by aluminium. During World War II, Germany and Japan recovered aluminium from kaolinite, a common clay, at slightly greater cost than it could be obtained from bauxite.

Due to the operation of these factors the world's economically demonstrated resources of most minerals have risen faster than the increased rate of use over the last 40 years, so that more are available now, notwithstanding liberal usage. This is largely due to the effects of mineral exploration and the fact that new discoveries have exceeded consumption. The real prices of most minerals have actually fallen over this period, as they have over the longer term[12]. The fact that we have, in this sense, more non-renewable resources than a generation ago is a major consideration in relation to inter-generational equity.

This raises the question of what might be the annual sustainable yield of minerals. With respect to agriculture, forestry or fisheries it would be possible, at least in theory, to quantify fairly accurately the annual sustainable yield on an indefinite time scale, based on the soil and water resources supporting them and inputs of fossil fuels and fertilisers. But with respect to mining, this would be a totally impossible task. Anyone who attempted to quantify the annual sustainable yield of minerals possible from the Earth's crust would find the question intractable.

For instance, how would one factor in the possible utilisation of the Brockman Iron Formation in the Pilbara region of Western Australia (already referred to)? Here, in one mineralised zone, we have 3500 cubic kilometres or ten thousand billion tonnes of plus 35 percent iron material which would be valuable ore in many parts of the world (much US iron ore is of such a grade). In physical terms this would provide the world with over 4000 years supply of steel at present rates of production, or it would build enough motor cars to stretch bumper to bumper right around the equator, each day, for the next thousand years. And all these figures can be doubled if you include the Marra Mamba Iron Formation 300 metres beneath the Brockman!

From a detached viewpoint all this may look like mere tech-nological optimism. But to anyone closely involved it is obvious and demonstrable. Theologically it is unsurprising. Furthermore, it is illustrated by the longer history of human use of the Earth's mineral resources. Abundance, scarcity, substitution, increasing efficiency of use, technological breakthroughs in discovery, recovery and use, sustained incremental improvements in mineral recovery and energy efficiency—all these comprise the history of minerals and mankind.[13] There is in fact a great abundance.

Sustainability in respect to minerals is thus much more focused on how they are mined and used, rather than at what rate[14].

Efficiency, Waste, Recycling

It can readily be seen that the role of technology applied to the energy and resource base that God has provided is part of his provision for us. In other words, that energy and resource base is determined by the technology we develop and apply. Only with the fulsome but careful use of technology will we be able to leave future generations with abundant accessible energy—not to mention properly meeting today's real needs.

The questions of efficiency and waste are germane to Sustainable Development as a set of ethical principles. *Prima facie,* it is more faithful stewardship of any resource to use it efficiently and avoid wasting it. This goes beyond economics to ethics. It relates to many, indeed every, way we use energy as consumers, but it also affects energy policy.

There are many who at the dawn of a new century see no realistic alternative to pushing Sustainable Development (SD) criteria into the front line of energy policy in particular. Whatever the seriousness of greenhouse concerns (which have taken on a political life of their own independently of the science), there is clearly more widespread interest than a few years ago in how we address energy needs on a basis which is sustainable for the longer term.

But SD is not simply about what happens in time. Its social dimension, aligned with that of Christian stewardship of the world's resources, is about achieving greater social equity today— meeting the needs of the less-developed two thirds of the world's population more fully and effectively.

Fresh, potable water is a resource which is clearly seriously limited in some parts of the world, but which technology allows us to extend dramatically by treatment of saline or brackish waters. With expenditure of energy, desalination of sea water can be undertaken.

The availability of mineral resources depends on a complex of economic and technological factors apart from mere geology, as depicted in Figure 1, and as illustrated by the story of oil and aluminium over the last 120 years. Even just looking at oil in the 1970-80s shows us all these factors at work, and incidentally yielding an abundance of gas! Looking to the future, it is certain that we will not be using oil in the same way 50 years hence, but neither will we be immobile! It is likely that hydrogen will have replaced oil in many applications by then. Overall, we have barely scratched the surface of the Earth in respect to the resources it contains.

A fundamental aspect of stewardship is avoidance of waste. The ethics of waste are neglected, though sometimes they are in one sense subsumed by advocacy of living more simply. But the more fundamental affront of waste to the Creator, beyond concern with levels of consumption that may be unjustified, is where resources are lost or misused with no benefit to anyone.

Recycling of metals is a major factor in their economy and utilisation. Reference has already been made to aluminium recycling accounting for about a quarter of the world supply, with steel it is about half, with copper 35% in the Western world, and with lead it is over half (70% in USA).[15] With aluminium particularly, there is a major (95%) energy saving in recycling.

Waste of mineral and energy resources can come about through lack of managerial or technical skills, through government ineptitude in regulation or in tax regimes, as well as in more obvious ways through warfare and natural disasters. In the mining industry it occurs when processing is less than fully efficient or when mines are 'high-graded' to remove the most economically rewarding ore and leaving behind lower grade material which could have been economically mined at the same time but which on its own may never be economic. This practice can be due to greed on the part of mine owners or to the structure of royalties and taxes. Either way, short-term benefits are maximised at the expense of long-term stewardship of the resource.

Waste can also occur through environmental destruction, perhaps degrading a resource by persistent pollution. But over-regulation can also be wasteful in requiring conformity to unjustifiably stringent regulations, beyond those required to maintain environmental quality and the safety and health of people. Often these questions are debated in purely economic and political terms, whereas fundamentally they are ethical issues to do with stewardship of God's creation.

Environmental limits require a properly informed and deliberate response in the context of the stewardship. Today the most obvious concern is the potential for global warming due to the inexorable increase in greenhouse gas concentrations, especially carbon dioxide in the Earth's atmosphere. While the evolution of this debate has at times drawn accusations of the abuse of science to create fear and advance political agendas, the state of knowledge now means that prudent action should be taken.

Limiting carbon dioxide emissions is the most obvious course of action, through improved energy efficiencies and progressively replacing large point sources such as coal-fired electricity generation with alternatives. Nuclear energy already saves the emission of some two billion tonnes of carbon dioxide annually, and there is the potential to triple this saving over 30-50 years. Wind and solar technologies, harnessing intermittent but abundant natural energy flows, will make a smaller, but important contribution at the margin. Already nuclear power is a major means of limiting carbon dioxide emissions in several countries, and France, Germany, Japan and UK depend substantially on it to make any headway with their greenhouse gas reduction targets.

An ethical issue for SD is raised by the popular push to use natural gas for base-load electricity generation. This is a enormously valuable energy source which is able to be reticulated to the points of use and burned there at high efficiency and it is also a magnificently versatile hydrocarbon resource, so it is doubtful whether our grandchildren will thank us for squandering it.

Long-term Availability of Fuels

As noted above, the measured resources are dependent on the intensity of exploration effort, which at present is low for coal and uranium but higher for oil and gas. Any predictions of the future availability of any mineral which are based on current cost and price data and current geological knowledge are likely to be somewhat conservative, and for metallic minerals such as uranium, extremely so. Figure 1 illustrates the dynamic interactions involved.

Coal is extremely abundant and reasonably widespread in the upper parts of the Earth's crust. It occurs in relatively young sedimentary rocks, often with admixed sand and clay. Much of the known coal is not as economic reserves, though it is accessible with current technology and under foreseeable economic conditions. There is no reason to suppose that there will be any significant resource constraints on the utilisation of coal in this century.

Gas is also abundant in some parts of the world, though present knowledge does not suggest that it is as plentiful as coal. Also its distribution means that the same sort of political and security of supply considerations as we have seen with oil since 1970 will apply increasingly. Scope for storage is limited, and countries depending significantly on gas and who are at the end of long pipelines are very vulnerable. With gas the question of opportunity cost looms larger than with coal, because of its versatility.

Oil has been under the exploration spotlight more than any other mineral resource, and it is likely that the peak of its rate of usage will occur before 2020. There is no suggestion or plan to increase oil usage in any major area, rather, there is intensive effort to substitute other fuels for it as prices either rise or threaten to do so in the medium term. Hydrogen is the main candidate as a transport fuel, but many technical challenges remain to be surmounted before it can be widely available as a substitute for oil.

Uranium is ubiquitous on the Earth. It is a metal approximately as common as tin or zinc, and it is a constituent of most rocks and even of the sea. At present neither the oceans nor any granites are orebodies but conceivably either could become so if prices were to rise sufficiently. The world's present measured resources of uranium, in the lower cost category and used only in conventional reactors, are enough to last for almost 50 years. Further exploration and higher prices will certainly, on the basis of present geological knowledge, yield further known economic resources as present ones are used up, and probably well in advance of that. A doubling of price from present levels could be expected to create about a tenfold increase in measured resources, over time.[16]

Uranium as an energy resource has an extra dimension. Whereas with fossil fuels the increases in efficiency of utilisation are incremental and measured in a few percentage points, with uranium there is well-proven technology available to enable a 60-fold or more increase in the energy yield available. Fast breeder reactors[17] can be started up on plutonium derived from conventional reactors (or from dismantled weapons) and operated in closed circuit with a reprocessing plant. Such a reactor, supplied with natural uranium for its 'fertile blanket', very quickly reaches the stage where each tonne of ore yields many times as much energy as in a conventional reactor.

An increasingly important source of nuclear fuel in the short term is the world's nuclear weapons stockpiles. Since 1987 the United States and countries of the former USSR have signed a series of disarmament treaties to reduce the nuclear arsenals of the signatory countries by approximately 80 percent. The weapons contain a great deal of uranium enriched to over 90 percent U-235 (i.e., about 25 times the proportion in reactor fuel). Some weapons have plutonium-239, which can be used in diluted form in either conventional or fast breeder reactors. From 2000 the dilution of 30 tonnes of military high-enriched uranium[18] is displacing about 11 000 tonnes of uranium oxide per year from mines, representing about 17% of the world's reactor requirements. Half of the uranium used today in US nuclear power plants comes from Russia's military inventory—it lights one in ten US lightbulbs. There is an interesting echo here of Ezekiel 39:9-10, where the people of God utilise as fuel the figurative enemy's weapons of war after God acts to remove the military threat: 'For seven years they will use them for fuel. They will not need to gather wood ... because they will use the weapons for fuel.'

Today uranium is the only fuel supplied for nuclear reactors. However, thorium can also be utilised as a fuel for nuclear power.[19] The thorium fuel cycle has some attractive features, though it is not yet in commercial use and only India (with vast reserves of it) is developing the means to use thorium as a nuclear fuel.

Nuclear Novelty?

Nuclear energy is a fascinating area for Christian reflection. Where little creativity was required for humans to learn how to burn fossil fuels, learning how to 'burn' uranium controllably was a technological feat of some magnitude, accelerated by wartime priorities focused on explosives. Yet in his creation, God had in fact done it already, though we were not to discover how until well after the first few hundred human-designed nuclear reactors were supplying electricity or driving ships.

The power of the atom epitomises the abundance of God's provision, because energy is so fundamental to providing for human need. Of course we must acknowledge that nuclear energy was developed first as an instrument of war, and arguably the potential for nuclear weapons proliferation still confers some ongoing moral ambiguity. But perhaps the same could have been said about fire and iron? Does misuse (if we call it that) at one time disqualify proper use in the purposes of God?

A more basic consideration is the proposition that there is nothing worthless in all of creation, and if anything seems super-fluous it may be because we haven't yet worked out its true purpose. With uranium, we clearly have an important purpose,[20] so in the context of God's creation provision it is obviously not redundant.

Then what about the hazards and problems of the proper use of nuclear energy, radiation, waste, etc.—are they sufficiently serious to disqualify its use? Despite half a century of almost totally positive experience,[21] does safe management of the nuclear fuel cycle require something more than we can realistically expect of our civil institutions? Certainly management of civil nuclear wastes is no longer an unsolved problem as commonly asserted—it has been undertaken safely and virtually without incident for half a century, certainly without harm to people or environment.

Effective technology for all aspects of the nuclear fuel cycle serving the 440 power reactors is well established in many parts of the world, and civil nuclear wastes are well managed in both storage and transport (cf next chapter). Just as in every other field, it is a reasonable assumption that that technology will keep improving, as it is with other industrial wastes (which arguably pose a far greater threat to civil safety and health). In relation to objections to the use of nuclear energy, people will always differ on what weight they give to particular questions and problems, while happily ignoring others. While acknowledging the lack of consensus, one needs to ask: what major natural resource and associated technology delivers so much benefit with so little environmental effect?

And if some are uncertain about the place of uranium in the scheme of things, then they are positively uneasy about plutonium! Some even see it as diabolical! While plutonium will not appear in any list of geological resources, it is clearly part of the created order and of God's provision.[22] Plutonium already provides about one third of the energy from a typical nuclear reactor. It has the potential to play a larger role in supplying the world with energy[23], and several countries are committed to moving in that direction, on ethical and energy security grounds. Plutonium is a superb energy source, not only in nuclear reactors which burn it, but also in thermoionic generators[24] such as in heart pacemakers, satellites and navigation beacons. Voyager's pictures from the further reaches of our solar system were plutonium-powered[25] and the Cassini spacecraft carries three similar generators providing 870 watts of power to enable us to find out the secrets of Saturn.

The first nuclear energy appears to have been generated about 2000 million years ago in West Africa (now Oklo, Gabon) in several natural nuclear reactors. The reactors operated there in a porous and wet uranium deposit.[26] The evidence of both fission products and heavy elements[27] such as plutonium is still there, and incidentally provides one of the clearest and most elegant proofs of an 'old' Earth.[28] In this context and in terms of biblical chronology the Oklo reactors and their products are clearly part of the creation process, predating humans (and the fall) by hundreds of millions of years. They are presumably therefore 'good' along with all the other natural processes which formed our planet[29] and which we sometimes find problematical. There is no warrant for placing plutonium (or modern nuclear 'wastes' for that matter) in a separate moral category to geological or other natural resources (or other industrial wastes). All need to be managed responsibly.

Today's concerns about global warming from a build-up of greenhouse gases simply underline the felicitous coincidence of virtue and necessity regarding the future of nuclear power, not only for electricity and uses such as desalination, but also probably for hydrogen production. This underlines the need to approach with intelligent respect what God has provided. We can perceive the doctrinaire exclusion of nuclear energy from some scenarios of the global energy mix as nonsense. In fact it is worse.

Understanding God's Provision

In the light of all this, it is fair to say that no human activity or legitimate aspiration has ever been limited by any shortcoming in God's provision for us. The limits, most evident in widespread poverty, are due to human failures in proper stewardship of the planet and its resources. It is human sin which causes war, exploitation and waste. It is our sin which saps the willingness to work and to create, to share and to give. It is our sin which makes greed respectable and which creates sterile selfishness by transforming proper personal responsibility into personal preoccupation and indulgence. It is sin which institutionalises privilege. The effects of the fall are ubiquitous.

But we nevertheless enjoy God's provision. God has provided all that is needed for us to enjoy the abundance of his creation.[30] This was explicit in the prospect of the Promised Land with its agricultural and mineral resources.[31] Just as the Israelites had to grapple with the practical questions then in order to benefit from those resources, so do we. Their technology was rudimentary but real and it arose from real but rudimentary science. Copper and iron in particular are not much use without the technology to smelt them.

Today our lives are even more technology-dependent, though it is uranium and coal which are the minerals under the spotlight, for different reasons. Technology enables us to apply resources as faithful stewards to supply people's needs, discerning as best we can what to do with the resources and aligning our efforts with our best understanding of what God intends.

Outright rejection of particular aspects of God's provision would seem to be niggardly and faithless. It implies that we know better than God what is good for his creatures and that it is very careless or even negligent of him to let us have access to the Earth's resources, particularly uranium.[32] Of course for public support there must be confidence in the management of the technology, and that can never be taken for granted as today's GM food debate in Europe reminds us. It needs to be a clear part of the democratic superstructure of society.

As noted, nuclear energy also has considerable political implications following the end of the arms race as military stockpiles are turned into electricity.

Chernobyl[33] played a major role in melting down the iron curtain and it has been a factor, possibly a major one, in ending the cold war and promoting a more global sense of stewardship of the Earth and international cooperation in achieving this. Who would have thought, in the midst of the Cold War of the 1970s, or even in the 1980s, that the substance of Russian nuclear warheads would be delivered to the United States—not by missiles but in shipping containers, destined for electricity generation? Perhaps our children will be able to look back in another fifty years and see that the use of uranium for weapons was simply a temporary aberration in human history, as people then more fully enjoy its benefits.

When Greenpeace says 'we have no option but to leave the vast majority of the remaining fossil fuel reserves in the ground' because of greenhouse concerns we can reject the basis of the suggestion, while responding to the challenge of using them sensibly and without creating any environmental disaster. The same is true for other energy resources.

God's gifts in creation far exceed anything we can get our minds around. We must not diminish them by our faithless attitudes, our unwillingness to grapple with their problems, or our irresponsibility. Nor should we unnecessarily diminish the mineral and energy options available to our successor stewards through our mismanagement or our failures in this generation.

5

Energy Choices

'I believe we have a God-given task of being good stewards of creation. For our fulfilment as humans we need not just economic goals, but moral and spiritual ones. Near the top of the list of such goals could be long-term care of our planet and is resources. Reaching out for such a goal could lead to nations and peoples working together more effectively and closely than is possible with many of the other goals on offer. We, in the developed countries, have already benefited over many generations from abundant fossil fuel energy. The demands on our stewardship take on special poignancy as we realise that the adverse impacts of climate change will fall disproportionately on poorer nations and tend to exacerbate the increasingly large divide between rich and poor.'
—Sir John Houghton, 2005

Chapter 4 discussed the resource base of minerals including some energy minerals. This chapter aims to examine the factors involved with choosing among energy sources, particularly for electricity, which is where the options are most numerous and the implications greatest. There is wide consensus that in this century we cannot depend primarily on burning fossil fuels, as we have been. Evidence for human-induced global warming due substantially to carbon dioxide emissions from fossil fuels is a pressing reason to move away from using them, and today has become a major factor in choosing among energy options. The future requires clean and reliable energy sources, and more of them than many have ever contemplated.

A major challenge for our future use of energy is to stabilise carbon dioxide concentrations in the atmosphere. This will require reducing emissions during this century to a fraction of present levels. Reductions must be global, and should be equitable. The Kyoto Protocol is an important first step in this, but developing nations must also become involved. International trading in rights to emit carbon dioxide will be one step in this, but here the focus is on how—in relation to fuels and the technology for using them— reductions are made in particular situations.

I recently spoke at a conference in Ireland which was focused on that country's hoped-for 'transition to renewable energy'. One delegate remarked later that it was surprising to see a representative of the World Nuclear Association sitting in a seminar on 'Bringing back the horse to agriculture'! I responded that this (for small-scale use on farms) was as much about appropriate technology as my presentation on the need for nuclear energy to provide Ireland's base-load power.

Originally, energy would have been an irrelevant abstraction—beyond what was generated in each person through their diet, or in a fire for cooking. Probably the sun's rays sustaining life through growth of plants was taken for granted or at least not categorised as we do now. Then the concept extended to what a domesticated beast of burden might contribute, or the sails on a boat which enabled the wind to propel it, or the sails on windmill which yielded mechanical energy. Meanwhile fire was harnessed for wider purposes including metalworking, and eventually making steam for other machines. Today harnessed and applied energy is essential to the existence of at least half of the world's six billion inhabitants, and on any reckoning it is central to the aspirations of the rest.

God has provided in his creation abundant resources of energy, unimaginable to those in New Testament times, or even a century ago. Of course some of it is in those forces of sun, wind and water which are long-known but now better understood and able to be more effectively harnessed than ever before. Some is locked up in the Earth's crust as fossil fuels, storing biomass energy captured long ago from the sun, and some is inherent in the more basic structure of matter.

How do we approach the stewardship of a resource such as wind or sun, in the sense of harnessing it? Stewardship of so-called fossil fuels (which are also chemical feedstocks) are something else again, and perhaps the stewardship of the elemental forces in atomic nuclei are yet another, if only because of the more sophisticated technology involved.

Energy Demand and Use: What is Sustainable?

There are several overlapping but key areas to be addressed:
• fuel for transport, particularly motor vehicles,
• means of generating electricity,
• fuel and electricity for domestic use,
• energy for industry.

The following focuses on electricity, which of course has application to the other three areas, the extent of that application itself being a matter of choice and policy, and subject to the economic and technological drivers outlined in the previous chapter.

No single energy source can be represented as "sustainable" on its own, we need to find the best mix appropriate to the level of technology and the competence of government in particular times and places, and discern what is best for sustainable development there. Some diversity is prudent.

Until twenty years ago sustainability of energy supplies was thought of simply in terms of their abundance or economic availability relative to the rate of usage. Today, in the context of the ethical framework of sustainable development other aspects are equally important: the environmental effects involved, the question of wastes (even if they have no immediate environmental effect), safety, and the broad and indefinite aspect of maximising the options available to future generations. There is no question that we do need to pass on to future generations a resource and infrastructure base which is technically and economically useable and which allows their needs to be satisfied as least as adequately as ours are, not to mention more equitably within each generation.

There is little dispute that the world's population is likely to keep growing for several decades at least, that energy demand is likely to increase even faster, and that the proportion of this supplied by electricity will continue to grow faster still. Today, worldwide, 64% of the electricity is from fossil fuels, 16% from nuclear fission and 19% from hydro, with very little from other renewables. There is no prospect that we can do without any of these, though we do need to push for more clean energy, without carbon dioxide emissions.

Opinions diverge as to whether the electricity demand will continue to be served predominantly by extensive grid systems, or whether there will be a strong trend to distributed generation (close to the points of use). That is an important policy question itself, but either way, it will not obviate the need for more large-scale grid-supplied power especially in urbanised areas over the next several decades. Those urbanised areas are growing. Much demand is for continuous, reliable supply, and this qualitative consideration will continue to dominate.

A forward-looking energy policy for each country has become essential with the advent of greenhouse constraints on top of energy security considerations.[1] The energy policy situation characterised as 'ideology, followed by crisis management, but no strategy'[2] is too close to reality to be funny in many parts of the world. There is little room for ideology in addressing world energy needs as a steward of God's creation.

Energy Supply Options

The criteria for any acceptable energy supply will continue to be **cost and safety,** the latter including environmental effects. Grappling with those environmental effects has cost implications, as the implementation of policies to counter greenhouse gas emissions makes clear. Supplying low cost electricity with acceptable safety and low environmental impact will depend substantially on harnessing and deploying reasonably sophisticated technology. While renewable sources are heavily subsidised today, as their use grows such subsidies will become less affordable. This was brought home in 2002 in Denmark, when subsidy arrangements for the development of further wind capacity beyond two particular offshore wind farms were terminated.

However, harnessing renewable energy is an appropriate first consideration in sustainable development, because apart from constructing the plant, there is no depletion of mineral resources for fuel and no direct air or water pollution. In contrast to the situation even a few decades ago, we now have the technology to access wind on a significant scale, for electricity. But harnessing these 'free' sources cannot be the only option. Renewable sources other than hydro—notably wind and solar, are diffuse, intermittent, and unreliable by nature of their occurrence.

Wind is the fastest-growing source of electricity in many countries, albeit from a low base, and there is a lot of scope for further expansion. While it has been exciting to see the rapid expansion of wind turbines in many countries, capacity is seldom more than 30% utilised over the course of a year, which testifies to the unreliability of the source and the fact that it does not and cannot match the pattern of demand.

A further, and rapidly-increasing constraint, is the aesthetic acceptability of numerous wind turbines on landscape (often scenic areas including national parks and similar, cf chapter 2). In the UK this is already placing severe, and perhaps terminal, limitations on the expansion of wind generation on land. In Europe large new wind farms are offshore, such as Denmark's 160 MWe Horns Rev wind farm,[3] 14-20 km off the west coast, with 80 turbines covering 20 square kilometres.

We can also make much more use of **solar energy**, for direct application (hot water etc) and to some extent for conversion to electricity. The fact that we can enjoy our summer holidays in the sun testifies to its low intensity, while bad weather and night-time underline its short-term unreliability. It is these two aspects which provide the challenge. And it is a technological challenge of some magnitude to collect energy at a peak density of about one kilowatt per square metre when the sun is shining and then apply it to the kind of electricity demand which exists.

Wind is clearly incapable of reliably meeting the main demand for continuous and large-scale supply, and solar is even less a contender. If their role is to be maximised they must be operated in close conjunction with plant which has hitherto supplied peak-load demand, notably gas and hydro. This severely limits their scope for contributing to electricity supplies, though that limit is some way off and there is an apparent consensus that it amounts to no more than 20% of total electricity supply.[4] In fact feeding such relatively unpredictable supply into an electricity grid system poses increasing challenges at much lower levels than this.[5]

The most widely-employed renewable source is of course **hydro**, which supplies 19% of the world's electricity now, mostly from large dams. The environmental effects and human displacement of these have sometimes been considerable, certainly building more is not an option in most parts of the world.

Beyond renewables it is a question of what is most abundant and least polluting. Today, to a degree almost unimaginable even 25 years ago, there is an abundance of many energy sources in the ground. Coal and uranium (not to mention thorium) are available and unlikely to be depleted this century.[6] Uranium is even available from sea water at costs which would have little impact on electricity prices. More significantly, the resource can be multiplied 60- to one hundred-fold by adopting the kind of technology which our postwar forebears thought would be necessary by now—fast neutron reactors used as breeders.[7]

With **nuclear energy**, now supplying 16% of world electricity, it was once assumed that uranium was relatively scarce, so much attention was given to 'closing the fuel cycle' by reprocessing spent fuel and recycling the fissile materials, thereby increasing by 20- 30% the amount of energy obtained from the original fuel. Today this is uneconomic, due to relatively low uranium prices and high reprocessing costs, but the dilemma remains: should we be guided by economics or ethics (coupled with the possibility that the economics might somehow improve)?[8] The question can be extended to consideration of fast neutron reactors which are currently uneconomic and await future resource scarcity to be widely justified.

Coal is an extremely important fuel and will remain so. Nearly one quarter of primary energy needs are met by coal and 38% of electricity is generated from coal. About 70% of world steel production depends on coal feedstock. Coal is the world's most abundant and widely distributed fossil fuel source. The International Energy Agency expects a 43% increase in its use from 2000 to 2020. In many scenarios, coal has been largely written off as a fuel of the future because of its substantial carbon dioxide emissions and the difficulty in capturing these. However, current proposals for 'clean coal' technologies may change this outlook, as described below.

Natural gas will remain a popular choice for many decades because it is versatile, the plant to utilise it is cheap, and it has less carbon dioxide emissions than coal. Development of combined cycle gas turbines over the last couple of decades has made gas-fired power generation very efficient. Today the fuel itself is priced to make it competitive, but there is major uncertainty about gas prices in the years, let alone decades ahead. Too much dependence on it either generally or for particular countries and regions is likely to create vulnerability.

Fuel cells are widely seen as the main future means of converting **hydrogen** into electricity, both for transport and some stationary purposes. They promise much but are still at an early stage of technological development with substantial R&D input still required. Their hydrogen fuel will generally need to be made from water,[9] by electrolysis or thermochemical means—the latter using nuclear energy, or perhaps through coal gasification (hydrogen today is mostly made by steam reforming of natural gas). Hence a very large increase in either electricity demand or in high-temperature reactor operation[10] is foreseeable.

However, electricity for this purpose need not be continuous base-load supply, and solar or wind generation may well make a major contribution here if costs can be contained, since hydrogen can be accumulated and stored. A more promising strategy is to increase the use of base-load generating plant, and the surplus power during times of low demand can be used for electrolysis. The safety implications of a hydrogen economy (such as might maximise the use of fuel cells) still need to be addressed in the public arena, though the increasing use of hydrogen in oil refining and its reticulation in pipeline networks suggests no alarming problems. The first hydrogen-fuelled vehicles using fuel cells are on the road, but not yet commercial.

Appropriate technology is fundamental to utilising energy resources, and it will become increasingly significant in any conceivable future. Manufacturing high-efficiency solar cells is not a cottage industry, nuclear energy has obvious high-tech requirements for reliability and safety, and today coal-burning is becoming a high-tech operation under efficiency and greenhouse constraints. Future coal gasification followed by capture and geological sequestration of carbon dioxide will be even more high-tech. Even natural gas requires substantial technological input for cryogenic treatment of it for storage and shipping in liquefied form (as LNG). Thermochemical hydrogen production (at high temperatures, e.g., utilising future nuclear energy) poses further technological challenges, along with those for storage of the hydrogen in motor vehicles if it is used to replace petrol and diesel fuels.

Security of supply is a major question for countries and regions. Arguably this requires perhaps one year's supply of any fuel to be stockpiled indigenously or at least in the region, as well as international diplomatic initiatives. Countries at the ends of long gas pipelines passing through unstable parts of the world have cause for anxiety.

Wastes Incurred and Avoided

A major concern when applying Sustainable Development or any other ethical criteria to clean energy production is wastes—both those produced and those avoided. The key question is: what happens to those wastes that are produced—are they dispersed to the environment, simply buried, or isolated more carefully?

Wastes do highlight a tension between considering as paramount the rights of individuals, both now and in future generations, and a more utilitarian concern with achieving the greatest good for the greatest number, both now and for future generations.[11] The first position will tend to lead to a rather 'precious' view of selected indignities such as radiation and nuclear waste, with calls for no expense to be spared in making these not only safe relative to other accepted hazards of life, but many times safer. Logically it should of course encompass all pollution and environmental degradation equally, and applied with common sense. The second, more utilitarian, approach will look at costs and opportunity costs and drive towards a more rational allocation of resources to benefit the poorer sections of today's population, while possibly giving rise to future risks (or at least laying itself open to that accusation).

With renewable energy wastes are mainly produced in manufacturing and installing the conversion equipment, with nuclear energy they are operational and in decommissioning, and with fossil fuels they are primarily operational.

There seems no reason why even intractable wastes from manufacturing, especially those from making solar photovoltaic equipment, cannot be dealt with. Nuclear energy contains and manages its wastes,[12] and the focus today is on greenhouse gases from fossil fuels combustion—most other wastes being retained in modern fossil fuel power plants. Nuclear power remains the only major energy-producing industry which takes full responsibility for all its wastes, and costs this into the product[13]—a key factor in sustainability. Hence with nuclear energy the waste question is political, focused on final disposal, rather than technical.

Electricity generation from fossil fuels produces substantial amounts of carbon dioxide, the greenhouse gas of prime concern.[14] As a rule of thumb, every thousand kilowatt hours (1 MWh) of electricity generated from nuclear energy avoids the emission of one tonne of carbon dioxide, relative to generating that electricity from black coal in today's plants. Natural gas contributes about half as much as coal from actual combustion, and also some (plus methane leakage) from its distribution.[15] Oil (petrol, diesel, aviation fuel, marine bunker oil) burned in transport adds substantially to the global total. As yet, there is no satisfactory way to avoid or dispose of the greenhouse gases which result from fossil fuel combustion. In addition many other wastes arise from fossil fuel production and burning, and while these may be controlled in varying degrees, they are still a factor which must make us look to a new era when the amount and intensity of energy use is not directly proportional to resulting environmental impact.

Burning coal produces about 9 billion tonnes of carbon dioxide each year which is released to the atmosphere, about 70% of this being from power generation. 'Clean coal' technologies are addressing this problem so that the world's enormous resources of coal might be utilised for future generations without contributing to global warming. The main such technology involves using the coal to make hydrogen from water by a two-stage gasification process, then burying the resultant carbon dioxide and burning the hydrogen.[16] Elements of the technology are proven but the challenge is to reduce the cost of this package of measures sufficiently to compete with nuclear power, with 'near zero emissions'.

Ethical issues surrounding nuclear wastes are topical, though all civil wastes are managed without environmental impact. However, prominence of the issue has tended to obscure the fact that these wastes are a declining hazard, whereas other industrial wastes retain their toxicity and hence hazard indefinitely. About 12,000 tonnes of spent nuclear fuel is produced each year, requiring management as high-level radioactive waste—a modest quantity for one sixth of the world's electricity.[17] Regardless of whether particular wastes remain a problem for centuries or millennia or forever, there is a clear need to address the question of their safe disposal. If they cannot readily be destroyed or denatured, this generally means that they need to be removed and isolated from the biosphere, such as in a deep geological repository.

An alternative view asserts that indefinite surface storage of nuclear wastes under supervision is preferable because progress towards successful geological disposal would simply encourage continued use and expansion of nuclear energy. This however is simply another case where ideological opposition to nuclear energy is more important to its detractors than dealing effectively with wastes to achieve high levels of safety and security, and further, ensuring that each generation deals fully with its own wastes. The wider question of alternative low-CO_2 means of producing base-load electricity tends not to be addressed, beyond wildly unrealistic projections for renewables.[18]

Of course nuclear power is not unique in having radioactive wastes. Most coal contains traces of uranium and thorium[19] with their decay products, as well a whole range of toxic heavy metals. Most of these end up with the fly ash and are buried on site or used in cement manufacture, but if emissions are uncontrolled all this is dispersed with the plume, and a coal-fired plant then emits more radiation than its nuclear equivalent. A total of 280 million tonnes of coal ash, most containing radionuclides, is produced each year, some being used in building materials. Natural gas is often associated with radon, and its production results in a good deal of fairly highly radioactive scale in the pipes, which is an occupational health hazard and the main source of radioactive contamination in the North Sea.

Given that radioactive wastes arising from nuclear power generation are contentious, the first observation to make is that they have been handled safely and almost uneventfully for fifty years. Secondly, they are no more hazardous than many other industrial wastes, which also need to be handled with care. As an OECD report[20] made clear in 2001: 'The scientific and technical community generally feels confident that there already exist technical solutions to the spent fuel and nuclear waste conditioning and disposal question. This is a consequence of many years work by numerous professionals in institutions around the world. .... There is a wide consensus on the safety and benefits of geological disposal.'

The only other point to make is that geological disposal (say 500 metres deep as generally envisaged) will put the high-level radioactive wastes well down towards the Earth's mantle which is already heated by the radioactive decay of uranium-238,[21] driving continental drift and helping keep the planet livable.

Safety and External Costs, Opportunity Costs

It is difficult to compare the safety of different energy source, let alone for any comparison to be readily understood and applied.

Ethical Aspects of Wastes

In an OECD paper,[22] Claudio Pescatore outlines some ethical dimensions of the long-term management of radioactive wastes. He starts on a very broad canvas by quoting four fundamental principles proposed by the US National Academy of Public Administration. This proposal followed a request from the US Government to elucidate principles to guide decisions by public administration on the basis of the international Earth Summit[23] and UNESCO Declarations which acknowledge responsibilities to future generations:

• The Trustee Principle says that "Every generation has obligations as trustee to protect the interests of future generations.'

• The Sustainability Principle states that "No generation should deprive future generation of the opportunity for a quality of life comparable to its own."

• The Chain of Obligation Principle says that "Each generation's primary obligation is to provide for the needs of the living and succeeding generations," the emphasis being that "near-term concrete hazards have priority over long-term hypothetical hazards."

• The Precautionary Principle is expressed as "Actions that pose a realistic threat of irreversible harm or catastrophic consequences should not be pursued unless there is some countervailing need to benefit either current or future generations."

These can be applied to the question of nuclear wastes, and in particular to their geological disposal, a system with inherent passive safety. In the light of the IAEA and the NEA 1995 publications on the matter, the principles in this context are summarised as follows:

• The generation producing the waste is responsible for its safe management and the associated costs.

• There is an obligation to protect individuals and the environment both now and in the future.

• There is no moral basis for discounting future health and risks of environmental damage.

• Our descendants should not knowingly be exposed to risks which we would not accept today. Individuals should be protected at least as well as they are today.

• The safety and security of repositories should not presume a stable social structure for the indefinite future or continued technological progress.

• Waste should be processed so they will not be a burden for future generations. However, we should not unnecessarily limit the capacity of future generations to assume management control, including possible recovery of the wastes.

• We are responsible for passing on to future generations our knowledge concerning the risks related to waste.

> • There should be enough flexibility in the disposal procedures to allow alternative choices. In particular information should be made available so the public can take part in the decision-making process which, in this case, will proceed in stages.
> Geological disposal is considered as the final stage in waste management, to ensure security and safety in a way that will not require surveillance, maintenance, or institutional control.

First there is the comparison of routine operations, in the absence of any accidents. The health effects here are a major component of the external costs (see below). Then there is the comparison of accident probability, which must be substantially based on records. Finally there is the subjective dimension of appreciating risk in relation to such possible accidents.

A major study from the Paul Scherrer Institut in Switzerland documents the accident comparisons.[24] The 400-page report was commissioned by the Swiss Federal Office of Energy. It draws on data from 4290 energy-related accidents, 1943 of them classified as severe, and compares different energy sources.[25] It points out that Full Cost Accounting, including both internal and external costs, is increasingly used for electric utility planning, though not on any standard basis, and not without considerable practical difficulty in assigning costs. Considering only deaths and comparing them per billion kilowatt-years (TWyr), coal has 342, hydro 883, gas 85 and nuclear power only 8 (/TWyr).[26] In terms of number of immediate deaths per event from 1969 through to 1996, hydro-electricity stands out with about 550 compared with coal at about 40. In the period from 1975, typically about 30 energy-related accidents with at least five fatalities occurred every year, including up to five with over 100 fatalities. Only one of the accidents within the scope of the study was nuclear.

Certainly any table of major accidents related to energy production shows up hydro-electric generation in a bad light—3500 killed in two Indian dam failures in 1979-80 and hundreds more since. But coal should probably be more in the safety spotlight, with many hundreds of miners killed each year producing (mostly) fuel for power generation. In China alone, over 6000 coal miners are killed each year. Then there are the health effects of pollutants from burning it—the external costs.

Relative to any other major technology, the safety record of nuclear power is outstanding, and engineered safety improves with each new generation of nuclear plants. This safety picture is notwithstanding the continued operation of a small number of reactors which are, by Western standards, distinctly unsatisfactory.[27] Over 11,000 reactor-years of operation in 32 countries have shown a remarkable lack of problems in any of the reactors which are licenseable in most of the world. Safety was given a very high priority from the outset of the civil nuclear energy program, at least in the West.[28] About one third of the cost of a typical reactor is due to its safety systems and structures, including containment and back-up provisions, for operators as much as for the public. This is a higher proportion even than in aircraft design and construction. Strict standards were set for the allowable statistical incidence of core damage accidents in reactors, and stricter ones still for any significant release of radioactivity.

The external costs of energy sources relevant are a major consideration for sustainable development, and for a Christian approach to stewardship. External costs are defined as those actually incurred in relation to health and the environment and quantifiable but not built into the cost of the energy or electricity to the consumer, and therefore which are borne by society at large. They include particularly the effects of air pollution on human health, crop yields and buildings, as well as occupational disease and accidents. Until recently it has been possible to consider only internal costs—fuel, operation & maintenance, capital & finance, and those waste costs which actually became part of annual expenditure. Nuclear energy has always had to carry higher internalised costs than its competitors simply because from the outset, waste disposal and decommissioning costs have generally been internalised via levies of some kind. But looking ahead, any generating capacity needs to factor in such costs.

Foremost are the implicit subsidies given where the waste products of energy use—notably carbon dioxide but also acknowledged pollutants, are allowed to be dumped into the biosphere.

Nuclear energy has always had to cost in its own waste management and disposal (equivalent to about 5% of generation cost, with a further similar sum for decommissioning). Renewables only give rise to wastes in manufacturing, and while these are sometimes unpleasant they are dealt with in the same way as other manufacturing wastes.

The report of ExternE, a major European study of the external costs of various fuel cycles, focusing on coal and nuclear, was released in 2001.[29] This was the first research project of its kind 'to put plausible financial figures against damage resulting from different forms of electricity production for the entire EU.' The methodology measures emissions, their dispersion and ultimate impact. With nuclear energy the (low) risk of accidents is factored in along with high estimates of radiological impacts from mine tailings and carbon-14 emissions from reprocessing (waste management and decommissioning being already within the cost to the consumer).

The report shows that in clear cash terms coal incurs about ten times the costs of nuclear energy.[30] The EU cost of electricity generation without these external costs averages about 4 cents/kWh. If these external costs were in fact included, the EU price of electricity from coal would double and that from gas would increase 30%. These are without attempting to include possible impacts of fossil fuels on global warming. Swedish utilities have also done some work on analysing external costs, but the point is that such costs are ubiquitous, and for fossil fuels, very significant.

An earlier European study[31] quantified environmental damage costs from fossil fuel electricity generation in the EU for 1990 as US$70 billion, about 1% of GDP then. This included impacts on human health, building materials and crop production, but not global warming.

A major ethical, social, economic and political issue then is: how and when will external costs, which we can now quantify with some meaning, be factored in to electricity generation? Christians may well be in the forefront of those seeking to have such costs internalised or imposed as tax.

There has been a concerted attempt recently to question the net energy benefits of nuclear energy by asserting that it requires so much energy input, and incurs so much longer-term energy debt, that it is not viable, and that the greenhouse gas emissions from those inputs and debts cancel out any advantage on that score. This question is fully addressed elsewhere.[32] The charge does not stand up, and in fact energy inputs on a lifetime basis are typically about 2-3% of the lifetime outputs.[33] The question of greenhouse gas emissions incurred in the energy inputs depends of course on the source of energy for those inputs, but the debate is more about sophistry than science.

Nuclear energy and renewables have one important feature in common: they give us access to virtually limitless resources of energy with negligible opportunity cost—we are not depleting fuel resources useful for other purposes, and we are using relatively abundant rather than less abundant energy. Considering these from a future-oriented perspective is likely to reaffirm the desirability of utilising such energy sources. It may also suggest that the time is not far off when fossil carbon-based fuels are too valuable to burn on the scale we have been doing (though coal prospects are limited more by greenhouse than resource considerations).

Sustainable Energy Security

The notion of sustainability may be expected to assert itself politically before it starts to drive the economics of fuel choice for electricity production in the way that has been seen with oil in the last three decades. The sooner substantial wind capacity is operating on grid systems the sooner its advantages and limitations will become widely and unambiguously evident. That will help focus the public discussion on the real options for clean base-load electricity.

Particularly from a national perspective, the security of future energy supplies is a major factor in assessing their sustainability. Whenever objective assessment is made of national or regional energy policies, security is a priority.

France's decision in 1974 to expand dramatically its use of nuclear energy was driven primarily by considerations of energy security, though their economic virtues have since become more prominent.[34] The EU Green Paper on energy security in 2000 put forward coal, nuclear energy and renewables as three pillars of future energy security for Europe, and this was confirmed by the EU Parliament in November 2001. The US government is clear that nuclear energy must play an increasing role this century, along with fossil fuel resources.

Recent analyses providing 50-year electricity scenarios show the main load being carried by coal, gas, and nuclear, with the balance among them depending on economic factors in the context of various levels of greenhouse constraints. Those scenarios aligned with Sustainable Development principles emphasise nuclear fission for large-scale, highly energy-intensive needs, along with renewables for small-scale (and especially dispersed) low-intensity needs. The alternative to such a dual approach is either squandering fossil carbon resources (along with exacerbating atmospheric carbon dioxide levels) or denying the aspirations of many billions of people in the next couple of generations.

6

Contested Ground

There is a profound clash between those whose negative outlook on resource and environmental issues fuels pessimism, anger or despair, and those who see positive improvements fuelling hope. While positive action can result from either camp, the contrast merits analysis, especially where it affects development issues and how we approach the faithful stewardship of all that God has provided. (Complacency is another option, well supported in some political contexts, but not commended here.)

In 1994 I was working with a colleague doing an environmental consultancy which looked at how land was managed in Australia to enhance nature conservation values.[1] As we walked through the denuded Hattah Lakes National Park reflecting on its lack of funds to undertake needed management he ventured the opinion that 'what this place really needs is a gold mine'. Coming from an ex-National Parks Service person, that was fairly radical. Our study identified proper land management (rather than the land's designation) as the key to enhancing nature conservation values, the corollary being that there needed to be some flexibility to fund this.

The contribution of the Ranger mine to Australia's Kakadu National Park is a prime example of an economic activity requiring the sacrifice of five square kilometres but funding much improved research and management on 1980 sq km of the National Park itself (the mine is actually outside it, but need it be?). However, on ideological grounds, involving a view of the sacredness of land defined by lines on a map, such solutions are out of court as far as the main conservation groups are concerned in developed countries such as the USA and Australia. Practical solutions are less important than the principle of inviolate National Parks, even if that principle means they are degraded and inadequately managed. That is the usual reality.

Challenging Conventional Wisdom

A UK TV series *Against Nature* in 1998 made the point that Western environmental ideology, emerging in the context of material prosperity and inflicted somewhat forcibly on the third world, consigns millions of people there to poverty, ill health, hunger and early death—or at least it conspicuously fails to help overcome these. The program caused a spate of complaints in the UK, but Britain's Independent TV Commission apparently found 'no evidence that it was biased or inaccurate' though some minor contributors (not quoted here) were 'unfairly edited'.

I recall the same tension being expressed at the International Youth Conference on the Human Environment at Hamilton, Ontario, in 1971. Western delegates were zealous for draconian action to counter current environmental degradation as they (we) perceived it. Third world delegates were insulted by this, wanting development first and getting quite angry about being pushed into sacrificing such aims for environmental purity. Twenty five years later, *Against Nature* displayed the same clash of values and the evolution of environmental programs under UN auspices also expresses the conflict.

What has changed from 1971? First, many Western gurus have become more ideological and less tentative about what they see as the way ahead. In the TV program Edward Goldsmith, Editor of *The Ecologist,* volunteered that 'There is no evidence that modern (Western) society works', and 'Our environment cannot sustain the present impact of our economic activities'. This shared sentiment made the several commentators featured all the more patronising of different, third world, points of view. The contrast was very evident in the extended on-camera discourse, leading to dissident Frank Furedi describing the resultant impact of Western environmentalism as being 'as intrusive today as imperialism was in the nineteenth century'.

Secondly, the third world views are much better developed and considered than at the 1971 conference, and the idealism expressed by Western greens regarding life in the third world is more strongly resented. In developing countries today, compared with 30 years ago, there is a much greater ability to conceive and plan development so that the environmental costs are properly factored in and minimised.

Thirdly, and partly due to those of us who paved the way for today's green ideologues, environmental quality in the West has, in many respects, improved greatly in the last few decades. Decreased urban air pollution and improvements in water quality are evident in North America and Europe—an outcome of engagement with these matters in the early 1970s. At the same time we are told that in the third world today 1.5 billion people experience air pollution which is 'dangerously unsafe' (e.g., five million infants die each year from respiratory diseases caused by indoor smoke), that 250 million are infected each year with water-borne diseases (causing ten million deaths).[2] Much of this could be avoided with appropriate development which has largely been compromised by environmentalist pressure on the World Bank directly and through Western governments.

Clean drinking water and electricity to replace cow-dung fires are the key resources depicted as being denied by green ideology; some 300 blocked dam developments apparently only 'serving greed' and causing 'genocide of tribal peoples' according to Lisa Jordan, head of the activist Bank Information Centre. Brent Blackwater, Chairman of Friends of the Earth, boasted that 'we were able to get rid of 150 unnecessary and environmentally-destructive dam projects.'[3] Doubtless some projects would have been as he describes them and there is certainly no lack of ecological disaster stories concerning dams, but other such 'achievements' and 'successes' appear to mean denying much-needed development. A local Indian leader calls one such obstruction 'a crime against humanity' as, allegedly, 30-40 million people are deprived of clean water, electricity and irrigation for food crops (after much of the project had been built!). There are both costs and benefits connected with any major project, but it is not clear that Western ideologues are best equipped to balance those on behalf of the people involved in developing countries.

But, some of the high profile green gurus of the early 1970s are still prominent in the public arena, despite the now-obvious falsity of their earlier apocalyptic utterances. On any rational assessment Paul Ehrlich[4] should be totally discredited and the late Julian Simon a folk hero, but Ehrlich is somehow seen as conventional wisdom and Simon an extremist. On the other hand, the originator of the Gaia hypothesis, James Lovelock, has conspicuously broken ranks with the environmental hard core and pointed out that 'the objections to [nuclear power] are unscientific and perverse' and we 'must embrace science and engineering ... to lessen our impact on the Earth.' We need genetic engineering for food, 'nuclear energy playing a big part' for electricity and more. If 'fretting over the minute risks of cancer from chemicals or radiation' means that 'we fail to concentrate our minds on the real danger—global warming— we may die sooner.'[5]

In 2001, Matt Ridley[6] in the Prince Philip lecture for the UK's Royal Society of the Arts et al took up the same theme. He referred to his background in Friends of the Earth and went on to catalogue environmental improvements which belied much of the continuing rhetoric of the green movement. Acid rain— once seen as destroying Northern Hemisphere forests, has receded as a threat, food production is growing remarkably, minerals are abundant and the human ecological footprint is not increasing at anything like the same rate as population. 'I suggest that the most powerful influence on how we treat our environment is not how much we care, or how much we pass laws, but what technology we invent.' Which brings him to the values clash considered in the Introduction, and the need to embrace economic and technological development in order to achieve ecological salvation—or at least affordable sustainability.

Misanthropic preoccupation with population growth leads to a counsel of despair, fanned by credulous media.

The Skeptical Environmentalist

Soon after Ridley's address, Bjorn Lomborg's book *The Skeptical Environmentalist*, was published in English and immediately created a great furore. Initially it attracted unprecedented critique in the main science journals, which in turn drew scorn from the influential international journal *The Economist*.

Lomborg set out to get his students to debunk Julian Simon[7], the scourge of Paul Ehrlich and associated environmental prophets. But when the students dug into the evidence, some radical rethinking occurred. His basic thesis in the book is that environmentally, most indicators are improving, not deteriorating, even if much more progress is still required. But the fact that most trends are positive means that further steady effort should be encouraged, and pessimism is misguided. He attributes the normal downbeat view of environmental trends to what he calls the Litany[8]— a list of unsubstantiated assertions or half truths. 'Lomborg's targets are green scaremongers and their credulous servants in the media. He uses the findings of scientists to press his case.'[9]

Does it matter if people are unduly pessimistic and ill-informed? Lomborg says that the Litany and its exaggerations 'makes us ... more likely to spend our resources and attention solving phantom problems while ignoring real and pressing issues.' 'If we are to make the best decisions for our future, we should base our prioritisations not on fear but on facts. Thus we need to confront our fears; we need to challenge the Litany.' That certainly rings a bell with nuclear energy! The frenetic push to address greenhouse concerns primarily by harnessing renewable energy sources rather than expanding nuclear power is another manifestation of distorted policy arising from such folklore (in this case the nuclear subset of it, which Lomborg completely misses).

The point is that the problem is due to the propagandising by environmental organisations, led by the Worldwatch Institute (as rather tediously documented by Lomborg), but with Greenpeace,

WWF and others in train. The Litany output is readily picked up by the media, because alarmist rhetoric is more attractive than bare science or long-run statistics. While Worldwatch and others publish good data, they tend to be careless with the facts due to 'ingrained belief in the Litany', and perhaps what others might perceive as an ideological bias.

In reality there seem to be two factors at work in what might be called a faith system: an ideology with many possible dimensions (neo-romanticism, anti-technology, anti capital /globalisation /enterprise, mysticism, etc.) which sets the tone and agenda of what Lomborg targets as the 'Litany', and the believers who uncritically or even naively espouse that faith because they are surrounded by others of like disposition and are given reinforcement daily from the media. Never mind the facts, certainty is the key. This is real food for thought for any concerned Christians, and flags a vital role for anyone who is concerned that truth should prevail over prejudice, starting with the way facts are handled.

One argument defending green alarmism is that if environmental indicators are improving, then people should not be told or they will become complacent or delinquent. Lomborg in touching on the moral aspects of his thesis rightly labels this argument undemocratic, and obviously it becomes the cause of major misallocation of resources. But one place I part company from him is where he plays down the influence of actual environmental problems in galvanising action to address them and to reverse any decline or reinforce the positive trends. He is dismissive of what I would see as cause and effect at several points.

So why did a book directed at the politicisation of environmental concerns and the debunking of green dogma and folklore become a *cause celebre* for academic scientists who for the most part are not called into question in the first place? Partly the answer seems to be Lomborg's position on climate change[10] (his longest chapter, of 64 pages), where he wades into science more than statistics and gets out of his depth. On fundamentally scientific questions one can readily be sceptical of Lomborg (a statistician), though generally his scientific data seems to be better than that of his critics. His view on the cost effectiveness of greenhouse gas abatement seems to be as good an opinion as anyone's. Secondly the answer may be because in attacking scientists such as Paul Ehrlich who fuel the pessimistic Litany and who are easy targets, he ignores those moderate scientists who have no truck with the green fundamentalists and who have more quietly taken issue with them already. This too is a cautionary tale for Christians, to counter the substance rather than the excesses of an argument.

After an extraordinary 11-page critique by *Scientific American* with disparaging editorial note (January 2002) Lomborg replied at length (33 pages) to the four authors on his web site,[11] to good effect. However, *Scientific American* threatened to sue him for reproducing sections of their text he was commenting on, so Patrick Moore, co-founder of Greenpeace (before its radicalisation) sprung to his defence and put it all up on his web site[12] then dared *Scientific American* to sue him (it didn't). Finally, in May 2002, *Scientific American* gave him one and a half pages to respond publicly, followed by a derogatory and petty editorial comment which greatly diminished my esteem of that journal. The attacks from *Scientific American* and others[13] expose a more fundamental problem, the eagerness of some scientists to spring to the defence of their admirers who promulgate the green folklore which in turn skews political priorities wastefully. It is not limited to Lomborg. Commentators have also pointed to the effect of maintaining a high level of public anxiety to furnish the support base of green groups and academic research on particular issues.

In his native Denmark, Lomborg was investigated by a peculiar and somewhat Orwellian Committee on Scientific Dishonesty. In reporting the equivocal outcome of this early in 2003 (though it did not find any instance of misrepresentation), both *New Scientist* and *Nature* seemed more on his side than his inquisitors'. In *Nature's* opinion (16/1/03) the Committee 'misfired' in failing to show any dishonesty in Lomborg's acknowledged polemic. A petition signed by 300 Danish professors said that the Committee's finding that Lomborg violated good scientific practice was unjustified and should be annulled. His chief sin seems to have been that people took him seriously though his work was not essentially scientific. *The Economist* (11/1/03) called the Committee's ruling 'inconsistent and shameful', and *New Scientist* (Fred Pearce 18/1) said it was 'unfair and bad for science', casting Lomborg 'as the victim of a green witch-hunt'. *Scientific American* remained unrepentant for the disreputable part it had played.

Professor Deepak Lal (International Development Studies, University of California) wrote in *Financial Times* (14/1/03):

> 'I have argued for some time that the Green movement is best seen as a religion: eco-fundamentalism. Your report of Bjorn Lomborg's travails provides further confirmation.
>
> 'The Danish Committee on Scientific Dishonesty has issued its *fatwah* against Mr Lomborg, like Ayatollah Khomeini's against Salman Rushdie and the Holy Inquisition's indictment of Galileo. The Danes also want Cambridge University Press to suppress the book, which is reminiscent of the book burning and intimidation of publishers of *The Satanic Verses*. I hope this will open the eyes of those involved in environmental policy debates to the fact that the 'scientific' proponents of the green agenda burn with no less fierce (though a different) 'religious' passion than those of other fundamentalists.
>
> 'By attempting to suppress free debate and any questioning by lapsed 'believers', not only have they gone beyond the proper bounds of science, but their activist followers are also attempting to coerce the world to accept their 'religious' beliefs, no less than the Islamist fundamentalists such as Osama bin Laden.'

Strong stuff! *Nature* then ran a sensible three-page review of the controversy in May 2003, which concluded that the emotive response of scientists to Lomborg had lost them much public credibility. In December 2003 the Danish Ministry of Science announced that it repudiated the Committee's negative view of Lomborg's work.

For the most part Lomborg, like Julian Simon—another non-scientist who shone helpful light on the same area, assembles data and looks at trends, notably long trends, which is unusual and refreshing where people are attuned to the latest shock/horror environmental alarum and half-truth factoids. His book's great strength is that it goes back to primary statistical data, mostly from UN agencies.[14] One conspicuous deficiency is that in some scientific areas he quotes insubstantial sources and bases his comments on them, which is certainly a problem. For instance in cursorily addressing nuclear energy[15] he does this— hardly a helpful analysis for a part of his subject that has its own full-blown 'Litany'. But on the whole he is thorough with assembling data, and that is where the book is so valuable in challenging the cycle of assertion, repetition, assumption and what is taken to be 'known.' One is reminded from another context about the truth setting us free.[16]

The fundamental problem for Christians is that critique of popular views can be treated as heresy, even if those views have a rather flimsy basis in fact. Such critique should surely lead to re-examination of the basic facts, not to a heresy trial in the media, in this case the scientific media. Lomborg's book, like Julian Simon's writings two decades earlier, stands as landmark in the contest of ideas and ideologies regarding stewardship of environment and resources. The publishers are said to have reprinted it 25 times in less than two years!

However, there are dissident voices from other quarters also, and the USA in particular has seen a disreputable attack on the science of climate change over many years. The 'climate sceptics' have been very selective in what they quote, and have, in my view, unreasonably disparaged the emerging consensus of climate scientists regarding the seriousness of climate change. Financial support from particular quarters may or may not have influenced this consistent polemic, but certainly US energy policy has been slow to respond. The US *Energy Policy Act 2005* starts to redress the problem, and US Senate attitudes have moved considerably over five years. Once again there is no short cut to resolve the question, for Christians concerned that truth should prevail, or anyone else. Listening, looking afresh at the facts and arguments, and a dose of scepticism all help.

Symbols and Means

A major problem with the Western green ideology today is that it is focused on symbols and means, not on objectives. Its conventional wisdom has the authority of religious dogma, and never mind if it is counterproductive for resource availability and environmental quality in particular instances.

An Australian issue of contention is the question of eating kangaroos. Due to large numbers of two common species competing with cattle and sheep on grazing land, and due to large numbers in some arid zone national parks preventing regeneration of native tree species, many thousands of kangaroos are shot each year. This culling is broadly accepted, but environmental groups are generally strongly opposed to the meat or skins being used. In the state of Victoria it is illegal to remove meat or skins from the property where they are shot. There have been active campaigns against stores which stock kangaroo meat. This is despite the widely acknowledged fact that kangaroos are better adapted to the Australian arid zone environment than hard-hooved livestock, and farming them instead of cattle and sheep would be a step forward ecologically. Here is an issue where eco-logic and the avoidance of waste are in conflict with the symbolism of commercially utilising a native species.

Both this and the other Australian example quoted at the start of the chapter show activist and political pressures which make much of symbolism at the expense of achieving environmental objectives. I quote them because they go to the heart of the problem. Rather than looking at actual needs of real people, especially those in real poverty, we have Western environmentalist leaders proud of their 'achievements' in preventing those needs being met. Brent Blackwater was one such on camera. Edward Goldsmith said 'we must give up the whole idea of economic development.' And why? To pursue particular principles which are fundamental to their world view, principles which they defend sanctimoniously on camera as being 'for the environment.'[17] This overarching moral purpose justifies all manner of unethical high-handed action. Even democratic principles take a back seat in the environmentalist crusade.

Conventional wisdom is comfortable and enables the sharing of warm fuzzy feelings, but it is awfully prone to being wrong, unjust and ultimately destructive. At one level the New Testament is a story of overturning conventional wisdom! I believe that the Western environmental movements are overdue for an upheaval which will overturn some dearly-held stereotypes and perhaps jettison ideological approaches to practical problems.

When Edward Goldsmith[18] says dogmatically that a world population of six billion (since reached) is 'ridiculous' and 'farcical', with this sentiment being echoed by others, it raises a few questions. Why should it be ridiculous? Are humans simply a plague on the Earth or are they somehow creatures in God's image? If resources are seen to be a problem, can't we work on that? Others would see 6 billion (or 8 or 10 billion) world population as a challenge to ensure that everybody's needs were able to be met sustainably. Any presupposition that they cannot be met needs the sort of careful scrutiny brought to bear by Julian Simon and others who are not on that ideological bandwagon.

A key resource is energy—why can't God's abundant provision be more fully utilised here?—yet key elements such as nuclear energy are excluded by the green ideology which is espoused. This then becomes a circular or self-fulfilling argument; you exclude major resources and then wonder why you perceive shortages, which may be more illusory than real. But more fundamentally, what is a proper response to a world population of six billion? Denial on a purely ideological basis of most development options for the poorest? Or assistance with substantial development? (and not merely birth control).

While the above discussion emphasises the impact of green ideology in the third world, the problem is not confined there, it is simply that the effects are more debilitating. If a mining or hydro-electric development is opposed and perhaps foregone in the West, that has an incremental rather than dramatic economic effect. Wherever green ideology is in tension with the global technocratic and economic world the same scenarios are played out. But poverty is no respecter of environmental values and nor does it in any way enhance them. From our comfortable vantage point in the West we need to be reminded of this, and that the sort of neo-romanticism[19] which idealises nature and the past is no use at all in grappling with today's environmental challenges—the greatest of which is third world poverty.

Allied to this, the ideological attack on industry—what one might call the green Jihad, is familiar in many parts of the world, whether it is Greenpeace campaigning against a well run chemical plant, the Wilderness Society opposing logging in native forests, or the Jabiluka Action Group attacking a conscientious mining company. At its extreme, the stock in trade is a folklore built on misconceptions, half truths and hyped-up trivia. It can, as a rule, readily be refuted, but is nevertheless repeated regardless, the insistence apparently conferring some veracity for certain sections of the media. All this would be harmless enough sport if the health and welfare of the next generation did not depend on truth and commonsense prevailing. The positive aspect of it all is that the industry and government positions attacked do in fact have to justify themselves, which some even now are reluctant to do. Also muddying the waters are tendentious reactionary campaigns sometimes associated with industry, pushing agendas which are equally inimical to right resolution of complex environment and resource issues.

Since Lynn White's (in)famous 1966 paper suggesting that Christian-based anthropocentricism was the greatest threat to the environment, we have seen a burgeoning of envirocentric ideology treating humans as the ultimate threat, rather than 'the ultimate resource' (to quote Julian Simon's book title[20]). We need Christian assertion of a proper stewardship which affirms the environment but does not place it at the centre of all meaning and purpose and above the issue of widening access to resources. With 'dominion' in Genesis 1 rendered as 'responsibility' we are some of the way there, as outlined in chapter 1. A proper theology will help put people, nature, technology and economics into proper and productive relationship. There is an urgent need for this, starting in the West.

CONTESTED GROUND

So What?

The purpose of this chapter is to raise the question of how should (or might) a Christian steward respond in the light of these conflicting values, viewpoints and assertions. The following points arise form the discussion preceding.

First, to clear some ground at the extremes or fringes. A Christian, it seems to me, needs to stand well clear of any view of resource and environmental problems which says that the situation is hopeless because it is so bad or because people are so perverse that it is no use engaging the problems. Similarly, there is a need to stand apart from any view of the world which asserts God's sovereignty in such a way that has the same result—'there is no point engaging the issues because God has it all in hand'.

Furthermore, a Christian will stand apart from any position with conflicts with a view of humankind as made in God's image, with the corollary that people should be esteemed and valued.

Scoping the question to where most of us are:

• God is sovereign, therefore don't despair or feel that faithful endeavours are in vain.

• We do have significant responsibilities, therefore take them seriously.

• God has provided for the whole creation magnificently. If we at times become preoccupied with the problems we must not lose sight of this, or it will distort both our outlook and our policies and actions.

• God's provision is of many kinds, including:

- The physical properties of the world which are able to sustain life, from the atmosphere which retains heat and provides oxygen, to the inside of the Earth providing heat.

- The physical resources of the world.

- The human mind with its ability to discern the physical properties of the world and their biological outworking and apply this knowledge to making life better for more people and caring for creation generally.

• The environment is at risk or degraded in various places and in some significant respects—therefore identify these, work out what needs to be done, and get to work on it.

• There are numerous ill-informed or exaggerated claims made about resource and environmental problems—therefore make a conscientious effort to sort these out from what are real problems which need attention, and don't get drawn into supporting them.

• There are many claims made about how to address real environmental problems, which claims and programs are simply special pleading for other agendas, usually involving a lot of self-interest by identifiable parties. Don't get drawn into supporting these either, at least without having those other agendas made quite clear and transparent.

• Christians are disciples of the one who said "for this reason I was born, and for this I came into the world, to testify to the truth" (John 18:37). Very often truth in relation to environmental care and resource use is hard to discern, but it must be sought. We need humility and wisdom in this, as well as science.

• Where one is able to develop an informed and firm view on some aspect of environmental stewardship, contend for it publicly but with grace and charity, acknowledging that those who disagree are likely to have sincere motives and that the kingdom of God transcends many differences of view on everything from politics to petrochemicals. No position is right simply because of sound motivation. Relationships need to transcend disagreements.

In practice, applying some of these pointers is difficult, because our knowledge and understanding is always limited. Also, whatever position we take on any issue we will find ourselves in company with others who take the same position for very different reasons. But that is life, it is certainly not unique to environmental issues and it certainly doesn't mean that the position is wrong simply because others hold it for reasons, or on the basis of values, which a Christian might disown.

APPENDIX

A Review of Meredith Veldman's *Fantasy, the Bomb, and the Greening of Britain: Romantic protest 1945-1980*

Meredith Veldman is a US academic who has written an insightful account of the roots of the postwar green movement in the UK, related to Romanticism. Her 1994 book charts the evolution of the Romantic world view in Britain and the factors which led to its expression in what became the green movement. She starts with C.S. Lewis and Tolkein, who 'used fantasy to articulate a romantic protest against the shape and structures of the contemporary world and to assert that humanity must renew its relationships with its past, the natural world, and the spiritual realm.' (p39) They 'believed that empiricism and industrialism threatened to reduce the whole of reality to its materialist aspects. They were horrified by the mechanical destruction of nature (or what passed for nature in the UK!) ... and by utilitarian assumptions about ethical conduct.' (p51) Lewis asserted 'the sanctity of nature itself, apart from any relationship with humanity.' (p65) For Tolkein, the chapter 'Middle Earth as a moral protest' says it all. These 'works of fantasy ... were taken up and incorporated into British middle-class culture,' (p. 94) becoming cultic in the 1960s as the protest movement developed.

The book moves to the popular reaction to Britain's H-bomb, seeing it as activist optimism that felt it could change the world. But this soon extended beyond the Bomb to the culture which produced it, with the vision of 'a world in which political and technological structures would rest on moral, rather than pragmatic, foundations. The pivotal Aldermaston March organised by the Campaign for Nuclear Disarmament (CND) became a ritualized form of this moral critique' (p. 137) It was also 'a call to return to a world of community spirit and human values' (139). But 'in their attitude towards science and technology most CNDers were reformers rather than revolutionaries, [and] before the 1970s CNDers did not connect the production of nuclear energy to the construction of nuclear weapons,' (p. 153) over 40% of them identifying as practicing Christians in the early 1960s (p160). 'Many in CND still had great faith in the scientific promise of a new age: hence the stress on releasing resources for the massive industrialization of the Third World and the advocacy of civilian nuclear power.' This then changed to a more anti-technology stance generally as the call to participatory democracy gained strength and there was a swing to the left. 'In the 1970s CND joined the anti-nuclear-power movement' (p. 204).

While 'traditional conservationists were concerned with protectiing amenities and conserving wildlife', the developing environmental movement of the 1970s was quite different and 'argued that correcting environmental abuses demanded far-reaching social, economic and political change.' (p210) Eco-activism emerged. 'The idea that industrialisation in some senses violated the spiritual sanctity of humanity was a strong undercurrent in the early Green movement.' (p213) Economic growth was challenged and the concept of sustainable development was promoted, along with 'the conviction that global ecological breakdown would occur if humanity failed to change its course.' (p227). This culminated in the UN Stockholm Conference in 1972, which was a high point for British environmental thought though the warm glow was threatened by the insistence of the Third World's desire for industrial development (p239).

Different streams of thought are charted with care, including 'the critique of bigness (which) lay at the heart of the Green protest' (p. 246) and which culminates in the complex example of Schumacher and his romantic quest. 'Schumacher sought guidance from nature. He condemned nuclear energy because not only did the technology involved in its production epitomise the worst of the modern age in its expense , violence and potential for irredeemable damage, but also the interlocking complexity of the ecosystem ensured that radiation pollution would work its way throughout the food chain' (p. 283). Apparently he did not make the connection between nature's 'continual recycling of waste into nutrient matter, (exemplifying) renewability and conservation' and the closed nuclear fuel cycle! He 'saw the environmental crisis as primarily a religious, rather than a technical, problem,' and in relation to the Third World 'Western aid efforts exacerbated, rather than alleviated, the problems of debt and famine.' (pp. 290-1) His espousal of small-scale, intermediate technology is well known.

The book makes sense of many disparate strands and traditions in environmentalism, ideas seen as fads and foibles over the last 40 years. It does not link directly with postmodernism, but provides a background for understanding it in the perception that 'community could be constructed only when the bonds between humanity and nature, humanity and its past, and humanity and its spiritual aspect were recognized and restored.' (p. 302) It also shows how 'in the late 1970s the fight over nuclear energy became a central political and social battleground' for the greens (p. 300).

This leads to how and why the green movement in the 1980s posed a dilemma for those committed to rational, technocratic and international solutions to the world's problems. The movement's neo-romantic core, its reaction against bigness, materialism, and the loss of human-scale community, together with its mistrust of political and economic orthodoxy, pointed it in a quite different direction. And if this weren't enough, the incredibly stupid attack on the Rainbow Warrior and then the disaster at Chernobyl in the mid 1980s led to heightened concerns and cynicism and ensured that strident protest was plausible.

More than this, the assumption of moral authority by the nuclear disarmament people has flowed on into subsequent campaigns without sufficient challenge from society and government. It has also to a large extent alienated Western green groups from much third world support and sympathy.

Notes

Introduction

[1] Measured by average per capita Gross Domestic Product.

[2] McNeill 2001 provides an excellent environmental overview of the 20th century.

[3] An excellent Christian exposition of it is McGrath, 2003, though his assessment of the problem seems exaggerated, his case seems based more on legends of Prometheus and Faust than on Scripture and his viewpoint is at odds with this book's.

[4] Hargrove 1989 argues that modern environmental attitudes are the product of 19th century developments in the natural sciences, and that the neo-romantic reaction now evident against science actually derives from those natural history science roots 'which were strongly value-oriented from the very beginning', and closely allied with the arts (p. 78).

[5] Sometimes understandably represented as 'the enviro-media propaganda complex' due to the alignment of values which leads to a preponderance of activist propaganda—which certainly has great human interest value.

[6] Including the sanctity of creation as made by God, see ch 2.

[7] The International Commission of Radiological Protection (ICRP) says that *for the purposes of radiation protection*, the linear no-threshold (LNT) hypothesis should be applied, which implies risks down to zero. That is simply a conservative assumption which is appropriate to radiation protection, not a scientific statement that there are in fact risks down to zero.

[8] Millisieverts per year (mSv/yr).

[9] Weart, 1988, in *Nuclear Fear* provides a meticulous history starting in the 18th century with the popular awareness of radioactivity and fantasy about its prospects. He develops a useful model of nature versus (technological) culture and how moral perceptions in relation to each are opposite. He shows how 'by the mid 1970s the nuclear controversy had become, for the most committed, an explicit battle of ideologies', 'the anti nuclear movement taking its stand on powerful ideas that were more and more widely accepted', including antipathy to economic growth and the notion that the advance of technology harms personal relationships. Due to the ever-present threat of nuclear war with the USSR, by the early 1960s nuclear fear outweighed nuclear hope for most people. 'An entire technology and indeed an entire part of physical reality .... was now regarded with irremediable distrust. Along with this attitude came new stereotypes of .... authorities as dangerous men not unlike mad scientists. The dreaded energy lurked not only within matter but within the human soul.' This distrust 'broke forth during the 1970s in the movement against reactors (in the USA). Civilian nuclear power had genuine problems, but these would not have inspired such furious opposition had there not been increasing misgivings about all modern civilisation, including its structure of authority and even its commitment to technology and rationality.' (p422)

[10] *The Australian* 16/12/04, *Herald Sun* 17/12/04, cf Chase 1995.

[11] Stott 1999, p141.

[12] Gregg 2000 presents a useful response to this from a Catholic perspective. He concludes 'Fortunately more Christians are becoming conscious of the dangers posed by the flirtation of some of their co-religionists with extreme versions of environmentalism, and are willing to articulate a vision of the environment that is not only firmly grounded in orthodox Christian and Jewish thinking, but affirms that free economic activity is quite compatible with such an outlook.' (p 44).

[13] The complications arising from sin and the fall are addressed in chapter 1.

[14] Perhaps they are sometimes attracted by a certain quixotic element associated with it.

[15] Chase, 1995.

[16] Kimball, A, in *Creation at Risk?* ed Michael Cromartie, 1995.

[17] Rubin, C, in *Creation at Risk?* ed Michael Cromartie, 1995.

[18] Cohen, 1997. The result is clearly seen in respective approaches to whaling—the Romantic tradition seeking bans, the Rational, favouring

controlled harvest. Cohen sees business as a major factor in pushing environmental policy formulation in the Rational direction, as in Norway and Japan, so as 'to regain control of the debate over sustainable development and to advance a new interpretation that does not undermine the essence of free enterprise'.

[19] De-Shalit, 1997.

[20] *The Age*, 10 August 2002.

[21] Sheehan, 1998.

[22] Non-Government Organisation

[23] Chase 1995.

[24] In *The Age*, 30/12/92, quoted in Paul Collins op cit.

Chapter 1: The Stewardship of God's Creation

[1] From *A Prayer Book for Australia*, Anglican Church of Australia 1995, Communion thanksgiving #5.

[2] 'Nature' is not a biblical term.

[3] Much has been made of God's commission to man in Gen 1:26 to' rule over' everything (to' have dominion' in other versions) but it seems quite clear in context that this means stewardship rather than anything more autonomous. Douglas John Hall (1986) makes this case strongly.

[4] From 1974 International Congress on World Evangelization

[5] This ignores a US aberration which celebrates environmental degradation because it indicates the imminent return of Christ.

[6] Most famously put forward by Lynn White, 'The Historical Roots of our Ecological Crisis', *Science* vol 155 (1967), reprinted in Schaeffer, 1970, which was one of the first writings in response and making the case that environmental abuse is the result of the fall.

[7] McGrath, 2003, who credits Nietzsche with accelerating the process. His whole book is a very thorough repudiation of White (1967).

[8] Collins, 1995.

[9] Birch et al, 1990.

[10] cf Mark 10:18.

[11] Christian understanding of all this means that in contrast with much of the OT social context, nature is not seen as divine. That contrast remains relevant today in relation to 'deep ecology' and some Christian environmentalism.

[12] This does not mean we should abandon concerns about the rate of population increase nor relinquish efforts to slow that.

[13] Osborn 1993 goes further and points to the rights of the steward of God's creation, not merely the responsibilities (p 142).

[14] Lilburne, 1989, puts this well: 'As creatures in the image of God, human persons must exercise a dominion fashioned on that of God. The image of God carries the highest imaginable set of expectations; namely, that one will live in relation to all God's creatures with the love and care that God exercises. Arrogance or willfulness are as inappropriate here as would be a cessation of God's care for God's creatures.' (p 49). Osborn 1993 correlates the nature of God's sovereignty with the appropriate expression of human dominion.

[15] The two verbs are the same as those used in the OT for what priests do in the tabernacle and temple (Ernest Lucas, SU notes for 9/4/02).

[16] Osborn 1993 also makes the point that Christ's priestly activity reverses the alienatation of the Fall and reintegrates humanity with the rest of creation.

[17] John 1:2-3, Col 1:16-17. 'If Christ is the origin and destiny of 'all things', then 'all things' have purpose, meaning and significance, which interconnect in him. Christ bestows value on all creation, visible and invisible.' Dennis Lennon, in Scripture Union notes for 18/9/03.

[18] Peacocke, 1979.

[19] Genesis 3.

[20] Most strongly in McGrath, 2003. See note 56.

[21] There is a good deal of discussion about this hubris, mostly from academics rather than practitioners. In my experience of almost thirty years in technology-dependent industries I have to say that the main motivation I have seen in evidence is a desire to solve problems and bring benefits to people as well as success to the team. As we were all employees, profit as such was not a motivation, and arrogant pride would certainly not have been an attribute contributing to any team spirit or function!

[22] G. K. Chesterton succinctly countered this with the assertion that 'Nature is not our mother, Nature is our sister.' *Orthodoxy*, quoted in Philip Yancey, *Soul Survivor* (London: Hodder & Stoughton, 2001).

[23] McFague, 1990.

[24] Collins, 1995, p. 145, representing the views of Sallie McFague. Panentheism is particularly defective in its Christology and hence in effectively dismissing special revelation.

[25] Collins, 1995, p146, discussing McFague.

[26] A number of Christian writers on the environment embrace panentheism explicitly, e.g., Ian Bradley, 1990.

[27] Moltmann, 1985.

[28] Berry 1996 suggests that it is typified by Charles Birch and John Cobb, but see also later footnote on Cobb.

[29] Berry, 2003, pp. 98f.

[30] McGrath, 2003 (pp. 133-34). Then, as now, 'nature' whose virtues were so extolled had been substantially altered by human activity. The inconsistency is significant.

[31] Ken Gnanakan, 1999, makes the point that 'pagan' (from the Latin) means people of the land, referring to animistic nature religions which are essentially pantheistic (p 23).

[32] Bruce & Horrocks, 2001.

[33] This echoes the experience of early natural history scientists, cf Hargrove 1989, p 80 and Berry 2003, pp. 203-09. I still vividly recall as an undergraduate sitting in a second-year zoology lecture on echinoderms and being quite overwhelmed with a sense of awe and wonder at what was described!

[34] 'The Greens represent the new world religion—a modern version of pantheism—whose fundamentalist church is Greenpeace. Their political strength springs from the perception that they are being true to values that, deep down, most of us feel inclined to accept.' H. Mackay, cited in Introduction. One should add that there is evident a missionary zeal to persuade and convert 'unbelievers' and sceptics who may be indifferent to their impending doom, as well as an apparent hope of ecological salvation through manipulating social institutions, notably governments. Nevertheless much of it amounts to little more than 'sentimental illusions about harmony and peace' (James Nash in Derr 1996).

[35] Tacey, 2000. Berry 2003 (pp. 216-18) has a useful section on deep ecology.

[36] Its most notable flowering was in German National Socialism in the 1930s where the virtues of 'Blood and Soil' expressed the need for identification with the land, and those whose loyalty was elsewhere and whose culture was seen to be pragmatically anthropocentric (vide Genesis), notably the Jews, were stigmatised as an infection in the system just as humans generally are seen by today's deep ecologists (Clark 1993). He goes on to comment that older Europeans are thus very wary of ecomystical propa-

ganda today.

[37] The creation story in Lewis's *Magician's Nephew* is wonderful.

[38] Tolkien's Mordor is a ruined land which was once something good, and is contrasted with Lothlorien where there is no decay or despoilation. (Tolkien, 1969)

[39] Into the humanocentric he puts those who emphasise stewardship of creation, including Teilhard de Chardin, Francis Schaeffer and Pope John Paul. Jurgen Moltmann, with 'his avowed panentheism' is the leading light among theocentrists, with James Nash and Stephen Clark. The ecocentrics are led by Matthew Fox with John Cobb and the process theologians. He mentions that Cobb's ecotheological paradigm has been very influential and that the resulting process theology represents a radical departure from traditional theism, being closer to deep ecology, and in fact amounts to ecological pantheism.

[40] It is necessary to differentiate what is set forth here from scientism and secular modernity. The latter has been well represented by Andrew Kimball in Cromartie (ed) 1995. He says:

'Modernity has its own dogmatic belief system: (1) Science will ultimately allow us to know everything, (2) Technology will allow us to do everything, (3) The market will allow us to buy everything. ... This is the real utopianism of modern capitalist culture.' Scientism is a recognisable world view, involving an unrealistic notion of objectivity, together with determinism and autonomous human reason (Bruce & Coggins, 2001).

[41] The Nobel Prize medal for chemistry and for physics depicts a scientist unveiling the female figure of Nature.

[42] Romans 1:20.

[43] Francis Bacon and many since have referred to God's two books, of Scripture and creation/nature. Berry 2003 quotes 40% of senior US scientists as believing in a personal God, the figure unchanged between 1916 and 1996, though other figures show less..

[44] Berry 2003, Alexander 2001.

[45] O'Donovan 1994, pp. 81-2. The quote continues: 'Man takes his place, which is the place of 'dominion', by knowing the created things around him in a way they do not know him.' And 'to know is to fill a quite specific place in the order of things, the place allotted to mankind.' But 'this place has not been faithfully occupied.' 'Knowledge will therefore be inescapably compromised by the problem of fallenness, the defacement of the image of God.'

[46] At public lecture for ISCAST in Melbourne, 27/9/03. By his account, prayer was as important as anything else he did over 25 years of research.

[47] See also the paraphrase of Genesis 1 in front of book.

[48] See Clarke, 2001 for a full treatment of what is skimmed over here.

[49] This paragraph is substantially from a 1998 discussion paper by ISCAST on *Creation and Creation Science*. The statement continues: ' The basis of ISCAST disagreement with 'Creationism' is hermeneutical, not simply scientific. We would consider that the interpretation of Genesis 1 & 2 (and of the many other references to creation in the Scriptures) espoused by 'Creationism' (Creation by fiat in 6 Days of 24 hours) to be neither consistent with appropriate exegesis of these passages nor to be consistent with the expressed role of the Bible. We would maintain that the Bible is not given as a source of scientific information but is rather an authority on matters of faith and conduct (2 Tim 3:15).'

[50] Arguably the two complementary accounts are set side by side so that no-one would be tempted to try and read either as scientific.

[51] I.e., regarding interpretation of text. Most of the biblical teaching about God and divine realities is metaphorical or anthropomorphic, for obvious reasons. In Genesis 1:1-26 we have an account similar in form but very different in substance from other ancient creation accounts. It has a pattern of 3+3 days in figurative language depicting God's creation of the realms of the planet and then the inhabitants of each. There is no problem about light, with day and night, preceding the sun! The church through two millennia has understood Genesis 1 as figurative, the literal six-day view largely dates from the 1920s. See also Alexander 2001 for a superb recent account of the wider issue.

[52] A notable example of this is in the writings of Dr Andrew Snelling, an Australian geologist, whose papers (1979-90) on the genesis of the Koongarra uranium deposit explicitly refer to an age of some 2000 million years, and in fact, make no sense at all without that kind of time frame. His reputation, with PhD, was built upon his science. At the same time (or soon afterwards, 1981-94) and while depending on his reputation and not renouncing his PhD, he presided over religious publications whose basis is a young Earth of about 10,000 years since creation and with Precambrian rocks such as described in his scientific papers being 'probably laid downduring Noah's flood.' This is a sad example of intellectual and ethical schizophrenia (Plimer, 1994). Snelling's two overlapping series of papers are remarkable. They presuppose quite different time frames, and he never refers to his creationist papers or makes any young earth disclaimer in his

scientific writings, nor does he ever reference his scientific papers in the religious ones. He held a senior role in the Creation Science Foundation (now Answers in Genesis) through the 1990s, so the quoted example is at the centre, not the fringe, of the movement.

Interestingly, for me the most elegant scientific cameo on the age of the Earth relates to nuclear energy. About 2000 million years ago several (at least 17) natural nuclear reactors ran for some 2 million years in a uranium orebody at Oklo in what is now Gabon. All the evidence is in place geologically, and because of the relative isotopic half-lives of U-235 and U-238 the phenomenon would have been impossible less than about 2 billion years ago.

[53] Ian Plimer comments that it is the ultimate reductionism and simplification of the world, thereby removing a very large tract of life. Nothing can break into this closed system. It is internally logical, but as soon as the system is enlarged, it is contradictory both theologically and scientifically. Its followers are lambs to the slaughter. (Pers comm.)

[54] Though some science, e.g., thermodynamics, is said to be based on observation of engineering technology.

[55] This is emphasised by John Stott (1999): 'In all their research and resourcefulness ... [humans] have been exercising the dominion God gave them. Developing tools and technology, farming the land, digging for minerals, extracting fuels, damming rivers for hydro-electric power, harnessing atomic energy—all are fulfilments of God's primeval command. God has provided in the earth all the resources ... we need, and he has given us dominion over the earth in which these resources have been stored' (p. 132).

[56] Alister McGrath, 2003, however makes a case that the motivation for development of technology aims to remove the limits set by God for human behaviour and activity, removes moral and physical constraints, and lures mankind to seek 'the powers and possibilities that are here associated with Satan'. Technology is basically sinful according to this rather extreme view. (pp. 79-81) He does not seriously address the case for technology as a godly and positive development.

[57] Nicolai Federov is credited with providing the intellectual underpinning of this view, though it more generally depended on Enlightenment humanism via Karl Marx. See John Gray 2002: *Straw Dogs* pp 137-9 and P. Josephson *Red Atom* for a much fuller account of the technological arrogance.

[58] Peacocke, 1979.

[59] There is some discussion about the extent to which we 'image God' in science, whether the concept has been hijacked to give secular justification to science and whether it is sufficiently Trinitarian. Those discussions can be pursued elsewhere. However, I remain convinced that this application to science-based creativity is appropriate in the context of Genesis 1 and in line with the clear meaning of it.

[60] There is an excellent section on Science as Ideology in Bruce & Coggins, 2001.

[61] Ps 111:2, NRSV. This is the key text for John Stott's book: *The Birds our Teachers*, Candle Books 1999.

[62] See e.g., Deut 8:10 in its immediate context.

[63] subsequent chapters will argue that while there are major challenges for us as stewards of creation, God's provision is abundant, though needing to be unlocked. I am tempted to put 'need' in place of 'legitimate aspiration' in this rhetorical question, but the challenge for the Christian is in fact to align his/her aspirations with God's purposes, and not to be constrained by the minimalist connotations of 'need'. I think this is enormously important as a faith position vis á vis God's creation.

[64] Lovelock, 1979 & 1988. A contemporary review of it by Lovelock is in *Nature* vol 426, pp769-70, 18-25/12/03.

[65] Berry, 1996. Lovelock did not propound this.

[66] It is important to note that Gaia is non teleological, and not embraced by process theologians.

[67] SD is classically defined as an approach which 'meets the needs of the present without compromising the ability of future generations to meet their own needs.' World Commission on Environment and Development 1987, *Our Common Future* (Brundtland Report). It may better be expressed as an approach which permits continuing improvements in the present quality of life for all the world's inhabitants at a lower intensity of resource use, so that future generations enjoy an undiminished stock of productive assets (manufactured, natural and social capital) that will enhance opportunities for improving their quality of life. (after M.Munasinghe, 2001). More broadly we can talk of 'integrating economic activity with environmental integrity, social concerns, and effective governance systems'—the goal of the integration being sustainable dxevelopment (IIED 2002).

[68] a sceptical critique of this is: David Henderson, 2001, *Misguided Virtue—false notions of corporate social responsibility*, NZ Business Round-table.

[69] Berry 2003, pp192-96.

[70] For instance, ideological agendas which run counter to rational courses of action now, but which are dignified by appeal to keeping options open for the future.

[71] Berry 2003.

[72] In some parts of the world, wealth creation beyond the level of the localcommunity is virtually impossible due to the lack of social infrastructure—property rights (freedom to own and exchange), security of contracts, law and order, etc. See further last section of chapter 3 and Hore-Lacy, 1985. In its leader on the 2002 Earth Summit *The Economist* (31/8/02) said: 'Virtually everything needed to help countries grow and reduce poverty depends chiefly on domestic policies—ask South Korea, China and even India.' It went on to stress the importance of the West removing trade barriers, including agricultural subsidies.

[73] A view that because God loves and cares for his disciples/Christians therefore prosperity, not suffering or hardship, is the norm for a Christian.

[74] See also last section of chapter 3.

[75] Deuteronomy 26:1-5.

[76] Hore-Lacy 1985 argues this rather more fully.

[77] Running out of World is a chapter in Berry 2003.

[78] This section is adapted from a review of Berry (ed), 2000, for ISCAST Bulletin 2002.

[79] See also Derr, in Cromartie (ed), 1995.

[80] By the Evangelical Environmental Network, and subsequently endorsed by several hundred church leaders (Berry, 2000)

[81] Sider, in Berry (ed), 2000.

[82] Berry (ed) 2000.

[83] See e.g., Calvin De Witt on 'Creation's environmental challenge to evangelical Christianity' (expounding the Declaration rather than commenting on it). This is in line with de Witt's contribution to the 1991 book he edited *The Environment and the Christian*, where he first sets out his 'seven degradations of creation', some of which are tendentious to say the least (e.g., species extinction at the rate of three species per day).

[84] Deut 8:9 makes very explicit reference to such aspect of the promised land.

[85] Beisner has written extensively, and his 1990 book cited in the bibliography has some valuable emphases.

NOTES

Chapter 2: Finding Space on Earth

[1] Chris Wright (1983) outlines Israel's relationship with land. 'Life without the land was scarcely life as God's people at all' (p. 49). 'Shared access to land and use of the land and natural resources of the earth is a basic creation principle' (p. 77).

[2] Remarkably, food production is rising rapidly without a corresponding increase in land used for it. See also following chapter.

[3] Biodiversity itself is interesting. How should we interpret our responsibility for the non-human aspects of creation, particularly for today's particular assemblage of species in a particular area (or on the planet) in the light of our understanding of progressive extinctions over billions of years before humans entered the picture? That is not to argue for complacency regarding whatever extinctions are now occurring, but to suggest some perspective on those that are not obviously attributable to human modification of the environment or other action.

[4] A digression. It can be argued that hindering the gaining of knowledge about mineral potential, by placing some land off limits to exploration, is in its attitude to knowledge not far removed from book burning in mediaeval times. A concept floated at a world wilderness conference in the 1970s was that countries should put aside a lot of land in conservation reserves—far more than the arbitrary 5 percent which was then a rule of thumb target—but allow mineral exploration, with the presumption of possible development, over virtually all of it. The suggestion was based on the assumption that conflicts would be more intense if conserved land area was less.

[5] This question is treated briefly at the end of the next chapter.

[6] Beyond these people-related notions is the ontological argument that land, or at least some land, has a right on metaphysical and aesthetic grounds to exist undisturbed and that we need to ensure this. cf Hargrove 1989.

[7] This does not mean we should abandon concerns about the rate of population increase nor relinquish efforts to slow that.

[8] E.g., Deut 8:9.

[9] Mineral exploration today is more akin to scientific research than to any other land evaluation procedures. It involves the formulation and testing of hypotheses, the testing involving patient interpretation of voluminous data, and high financial expenditure in collecting that data. Geological theories evolve and the associated technology improves so that the passage

of a decade may give rise to whole new set of opportunities in relation to discovering hidden mineralisation under a particular area of land.

[10] Ventilation would be the main problem and might require some unobtrusive surface structures immediately above the workings.

[11] An orebody is a mineral deposit of sufficient grade, size and accessibility to have commercial value. In the course of thus defining it, a considerable amount of money may need to be spent—well over $200 million is not unusual.

[12] That proposal has been superceded by one to truck the ore 22 km south to Ranger for treatment, which means that instead of having some 160 hectares disturbed, with tailings dam, only 80 hectares is involved—20 ha for the mine and the balance for the road. It is this revised proposal with a much lower environmental impact which is subject to Aboriginal veto. The company is free to proceed with the higher-impact proposal any time.

[13] The relevant arguments having been thoroughly considered in the approval process spanning 25 years.

[14] Chris Davey 2002, personal communication. A mining licence issued by the state is qualified and contingent. It is not an absolute right, but involves a responsibility to serve the common good. It then confers an exclusive right to exploit the resource, but contingent upon doing something with it (work requirements ensure that a deposit cannot be tied up unproductively to the detriment of the owners—the citizens of the state concerned).

[15] The term implies placement in engineered voids 500 metres or more underground, maybe backfilled, as distinct from burial which has a near-surface connotation.

[16] Multiple barriers to mobility include having the wastes in a stable ceramic solid form, and containing them in at least one layer of corrosion-resistant metal.

[17] Hargrove 1989 notes that 'Wildness has been regarded as the special characteristic that sets the natural beauty of American scenery apart from that of Europe' (p 82).

[18] The Gila Wilderness Reserve in USA. Leopold spent much of his life devising management principles which he later disavowed in favour of a hands-off approach to ecosystems, or 'environmental therapeutic nihilism' (Hargrove 1989).

[19] Jeeves & Berry 1998, p228.

[20] Lamington NP and Cradle Mountain-Lake St Clair NP, 1915 and

1921.

[21] Roderick Nash (1989, 1990) in *The Rights of Nature* shows how Leopold extended the concept of rights to nature. His chapter on the religious aspect of this however excludes mainstream Christian thought. His opinion essay in *New Scientist* 30/3/02 starts: 'My purpose is to persuade you that wilderness is a moral resource.'

[22] Times, 22/4/02.

[23] John Vidal, *Guardian*, reprinted in *The Age* 3/1/02.

[24] Marcus Colchester, in response to Roderick Nash, New Scientist 27/4/02

[25] John Kerin, *ATSE Focus*, June 2002.

[26] Graham White, *IPA Review*, March 2003 p6.

[27] Hore-Lacy, I. & Parr-Smith, G., 1995.

[28] Berry, (ed) 2000, *The Care of Creation.*

Chapter 3: The Fruit of the Earth

[1] Lomborg 2001, ch. 19, 1961 data from FAO. McNeill 2001 shows fivefold increase in pasture 1700 to 1960 and almost the same for cropland, with shrinkage of grassland to almost half.

[2] Lomborg 2001. McNeill 2001 shows 19% increase in cropland and 26% increase in pasture 1960 to 1990.

[3] The Haber-Bosch process, the culmination of years of research, is fundamental to providing fertilisers for agriculture in many parts of the world. Cf., Vaclav Smil, *Enriching the Earth*, MIT Press, 2000. Fritz Haber was awarded the Nobel Prize for Chemistry in 1919 for creating 'an exceedingly important means of improving the standards of agriculture and the well-being of mankind', which now looks like a considerable understatement.

[4] Mechanisation is arguably more an economic benefit and necessarily ancillary to the fertiliser and pesticide (insecticide, fungicide & herbicide) application.

[5] FAO, quoted in Lomborg 2001.

[6] FAO, depending on government-supplied estimates, quoted in Lomborg 2001.

[7] McNeill 2001 reports a decline in Africa's per capita food production since 1960.

[8] ABARE, in Alan Moran, *Can development be environmentally sustainable?*, IPA, March 2002.

[9] McNeill 2001 defines the Green Revolution as a technical and managerial package exported from the First World to the Third, beginning in the 1940s but making its major impact in the 1960s and 1970s, centred on new high-yielding strains of staple crops.

[10] *Against Nature* TV series, cf Chapter 6. Professor Borlaug, who had tried to transfer high-yield farming techniques to Africa, was shown telling a US Congressional hearing how this opposition made him 'angry and sick'.

[11] McNeill 2001,p214.

[12] Lomborg 2001, ch 19, quoting Smil and others. McNeill 2001 quotes a figure of nearly 150 million tonnes of artificial fertilisers used in 1990, supporting perhaps a third of the world's population.

[13] McNeill 2001 makes the point that fertiliser use has so far masked the effects of widespread soil erosion and soil degradation.

[14] from 1961 to 1992 the yield in 93 developing countries of wheat increased by a factor of 2.7 to 2.36 kg/ha, maize by 2.2 to 2.53 kg/ha, and rice 1.9 to 3.46 kg/ha. McNeill 2001, p223.

[15] McNeill 2001, p222.

[16] Lomborg 2001.

[17] Bruce & Horrocks 2001, ch 6.

[18] Lomborg 2001.

[19] Originally Zebu cattle (*Bos indicus*) from India were taken to USA and crossed with European lines (*Bos taurus*) to produce the 'Brahmans', which were then introduced to Australia in 1933. They became widely accepted in the 1950s in both the USA and Australia, and breeds such as Santa Gertrudis, Beefmaster, Droughtmaster, etc became established.

[20] Peter Schmidt, pers. comm. May 2002.

[21] Jamie Allen, pers comm. June 2002.

[22] Heinrichs 1998, in Lomborg 2001.

[23] Jamie Allen, pers comm. June 2002. Drenching is the process of administering doses of liquid down an animal's throat. Dipping is the external administration of pesticide to an animal by submerging or spraying it.

[24] Vaclav Smil is quoted in *New Scientist* 18/5/02 (farming supplement) as saying that if farmers worldwide gave up their 80 million tonnes per year of synthetic fertilisers, grain production would fall by at least half.

[25] USDA & FAO, in Lomborg 2001. The world increase in grain production over the 40 years was 760 to 1860 Mt/yr, that in developing countries 350 to 1000 Mt/yr (Lomborg ch 9). See also note 14.

[26] Smil 1998, in Lomborg 2001.

[27] McNeill 2001, pp. 246-252.

[28] McNeill 2001, p. 247.

[29] In developed countries much of the paper fibre demand has been met using woodchip by-product from areas logged for structural timber. In Victoria, no area is cut for woodchips alone, unless one counts thinnings (Peter Fagg, pers.comm 2002).

[30] Sir Ghillean Prance, paper to Christians in Science conference, 1/10/05. See also W.F.Laurance in *New Scientist* 15/10/05, pp. 34-39: Since 1960 Amazon population has grown from 2 to 20 million, and since 1990 cattle there have increased from 20 to 60 million and soybean cultivation from 10 to 20 million hectares, supporting exports of about US$ 10 billion per year which help to service the country's $250 billion foreign debt.

[31] considering land units of tens of square kilometres. Areas not clear felled should include old trees as well as vegetation along creeks, thus maintaining diverse habitat over some of the area.

[32] FAO, depending on government-supplied estimates which are dubious definitionally, in Lomborg 2001.

[33] M.S.Filho, International Tropical Timber Organisation, Jack Westoby Lecture, Australian National University, 2001. Kofi Annan, UN Secretary General, is quoted as saying that world forest loss is at 14.6 million hectares per year, or 4% in a decade. *New Scientist* Earth Summit feature 17/8/02.

[34] Houghton 2004, p175.

[35] In Australia a lot of timber for house construction, and also wood fibre, comes from *Pinus radiata*, a North American species whose stands are practically an ecological desert in the local context.

[36] FAO (two estimates) in Lomborg 2001.

[37] Even in Australia it has now reached about 50% (Peter Fagg, pers. comm. 2002)

[38] M.S.Filho, ibid.

[39] I could take anyone to several places where I would defy them to pick the difference between virgin forest and rehabilitated areas which had been dug up a mere 30 years earlier to a depth of tens of metres. A problem for the industry is that these are invisible to its critics, whereas failed (or non existent) rehabilitation is glaringly obvious.

[40] 'Mining', in practical land use terms, means many very different things. Extensive mining such as for bauxite or mineral sands involves the complete destruction of ecosystems over relatively wide areas, but with rehabilitation following within a couple of years and hence the possibility of re-using topsoil stripped from in front of the operation immediately behind it, along with other plant matter. Rehabilitation is typically very effective. Open cut mining in a progressively-dug pit involves generation of waste rock, which can be emplaced with a view to its final rehabilitation. Sometimes, e.g., at Nabarlek and Ranger in the Northern Territory, the mined-out pit is used for emplacing the tailings and possibly also much of the waste rock, so that the final land form is identical to the original. In other places open pits may be left or turned into lakes, and waste rock shaped into compatible landforms. Underground mining involves relatively little surface disturbance (save for infrastructure) and simply some waste rock to be rehabilitated. Some are relatively long-term operations (>100 years). All of these first three types of mining are likely to involve some kind of tailings, which must also be properly secured and rehabilitated. In situ leach (ISL) mining involves very little surface disturbance beyond a lot of bores which are finally capped, and a lot of pipes across the surface while operational, typically for less than a year in any particular part of the wellfield. It is scarcely necessary to rehabilitate the land surface—much of the original vegetation can remain intact. The groundwater needs to be left in a condition fit for its original use.

[41] The Australian Minerals Industry *Code for Environmental Management* binds company signatories to first-world standards wherever they operate, so the alternatives mentioned are not available.

[42] McNeill 2001 has extensive accounts of water use and misuse.

[43] McNeill 2001.

[44] A 2002 international conference in Morocco on providing water from desalination affirmed nuclear energy as the best (and only non-greenhouse) option for producing fresh water on a large scale from salt or polluted water. The Conference organisers included the IAEA and World Water Council.

[45] This section draws heavily from Royal Society 1998 & 2000, and Bruce & Horrocks 2001. The latter is recommended for readers who want more detail than here.

[46] 'The insertion of specific genetic material using recombinant DNA technology'. Royal Society 2002.

[47] Bruce & Horrocks 2001, J.Peacock 2003 in *Australasian Science*,

October, pp. 23-26, J Marohasy in *IPA Review,* March 2004.

[48] GM crops are defined as those 'in which genes have been added, transferred or disabled in a laboratory using the methods of molecular genetics rather than selective breeding.' Bruce & Horrocks 2001.

[49] Study of 157 farms in 3 states published in *Science* Feb '03 and reported in *The Times* 7/2/03. In Australia Bt-cotton requires less than half as much pesticide as normal, and 90% reduction is in sight. It was the only GM crop grown commercially in Australia as of early 2003.

[50] *Financial Times* in *The Australian* 25/6/05.

[51] Partly due to the introduction of GM maize and soybeans which survive glyphosate, tilling (including ploughing) has been reduced or stopped on 35% of US arable land in the decade to 2002, according to *New Scientist* 18/5/02 (farming supplement).

[52] However, in 2004 four southeastern states announced moratoriums on it.

[53] 'Those who are morally opposed to this research [on GM animals] attempt to impose on the rest of society their views that GM technology is a sinister new twist in humanity's quest to conquer nature. Even so, most people recognise that we have been genetically engineering animals for thousands of years by selective breeding, and that this has been essential to our own progress. The new technologies of genetic modification are much more precise and should help scientists to avoid many adverse effects on animal welfare.' Royal Society 10/6/02.

[54] *Financial Times* in *The Australian* 25/6/05.

[55] Bruce & Horrocks 2001.

[56] J.Peacock 2003 points out the anomaly of a barley type with favourable characteristics. It had identically been produced both by GM and selective breeding but the former strains were not allowed to be marketed. *Australasian Science,* October, pp. 23-26.

[57] US$ 5 to 30 million to get regulatory clearance for each GM crop, according to *New Scientist* 18/5/02 (farming supplement).

[58] Beyond the ideological aspects, opposition in UK arose significantly from a flawed report that GM potatoes fed to rats made them ill, giving rise to health fears about GM foods generally. Debate in Europe and Australia since has focused on 'largely bogus personal health risks rather than the far more substantial social, economic and environmental issues.' *New Scientist* 4/1/03.

[59] Royal Society 2000, 3.10.

[60] Bruce & Horrocks 2001, conclusions

[61] *Times* 29/11/02.

[62] *Times* 4/8/03, reporting the announcement of a major Vatican report on biotechnology.

[63] National Academies, July 2004, *Safety of Genetically Engineered Foods.*

[64] Americium-241 in smoke detectors is a decay product of plutonium-241 which is one of the Pu isotopes formed in a nuclear power reactor (ultimately from uranium-238).

[65] though I disagree with the negative tone of their reflections.

[66] According to FAO, one in seven people are chronically malnourished, including one in three children, of whom 100 million suffer from vitamin A deficiency. About 400 million women of child-bearing age suffer from iron deficiency. Bruce & Horrocks 2001.

[67] All this is discussed very helpfully by Hernando de Soto 2001. He draws on the historical development of structures in today's wealthy countries and says that 'capitalist apartheid will inevitably continue until we come to terms with the critical flaw in many countries' legal and political systems that prevents the majority from entering the formal property system.' He says that the most basic deficiencies in many countries are ignored—'most people cannot participate in an expanded market because they do not have access to a legal property rights system that represents their assets in a manner which makes them widely transferable and fungible, that allows them to be encumbered and permits their owners to be held accountable. So long as the assets of the majority are not properly documented and tracked ... they are invisible and sterile in the market place.' Thus any market economy is very limited and capitalism is stillborn.

[68] Europe's Common Agricultural Policy dates from 1962, though it evolved from a 1957 agreement to boost food production at a time of food shortages. It was initially effective but by the 1980s was creating surpluses which could not be used. Reforms in 1992 and 1999 curbed some excesses. US farm policy with subsidies of US$ 170 billion over ten years has similar problems and in the light of US rhetoric on trade liberalisation, is particularly hypocritical as well. The 2002 US Farm Bill raised subsidies substantially. According to OECD figures published in 2004, European farmers receive 35% of their incomes from subsidies, US farmers 20% and Japanese farmers 58%, compared with Australian farmers 4%. European agricultural subsidies cost 3% of EU GDP, US ones 1.5% of US GDP (*Financial Times* 6/11/02). Some £28 billion pa in direct CAP aid is paid to EU farmers and

the cost of CAP to EU consumers in higher food prices is estimated at £33 billion per year. (*Times* 22/1/04, citing DEFRA and Oxfam) The effect of such payments on the rational production and marketing of food world-wide is great and grievous.

[69] World Bank report, quoted in *Times* editorial 28/8/02, gave the figure of US$ 350 billion per year—'roughly equal to the total GNP for all of sub-Saharan Africa', and seven times what the developed countries spend on aid. The EU External Relations Commissioner has said that it is morally wrong for Europeans to spend more on their cows than on the world's poor. *Times* 27/11/02.

[70] *Times* 28/6/02.

[71] *Times* 15/1/03.

[72] A bizarre example, with obvious implications for developing countries (and Australia) with efficient production from sugar cane in subtropical areas: 'By keeping Europe's sugar prices at almost three times world market levels, the Common Agricultural Policy makes the EU the world's largest exporter of white sugar, despite being one of the highest cost producers. The extra sugar which cannot be consumed within Europe is dumped in developing countries at far below the cost of production.' The EU sugar subsidy involves 140% tariffs on African imports and costs EU consumers and taxpayers over US$ 1.6 billion per year. *Times* leader 28/8/02, *Economist* 31/8/02.

[73] The US Treasury Secretary has suggested that if all trade barriers were removed, world economic output would increase by some US$ 2000 billion per year (*Times* 27/11/02). However, the utopian vision of free trade needs to be qualified by some consideration of national security of supply. For instance if all UK food were to be imported from far away on purely economic criteria, that vulnerability might be unacceptable to its government and citizens.

[74] About one fifth of the world's people rely on unsafe water and about half do not have adequate sanitation. *New Scientist* Earth Summit feature, 17/8/02

[75] IIED 2002, p. 20.

Chapter 4: Mineral and Energy Resources

[1] It can be argued that conventional wisdom, when hyped up to assert imminent environmental catastrophe, is rooted in unbelief and nourished on the same kind of hubris as that of the technological utopians.

[2] Details of the wager are in Simon 1996, p. 35. Minerals selected by Ehrlich were chrome, copper, nickel, tin and tungsten, and the period nominated by him was ten years.

[3] Meadows et al., 1972.

[4] In 2002-03, some 187 million tonnes of high-grade iron ore was produced and most of it exported, the exports being worth US$ 3.7 billion.

[5] In the first half of the 20th century, world production of aluminium doubled every 9 years, then from 1950 to 1970 it increased tenfold to 10 million tonnes per year as it started to be used for drink cans. Magnesium and titanium are following aluminium in technology-enabled availability. (Ridley 2001, IIED 2002) Interestingly, the 25 Mt would require a minimum of 350 billion kWh to smelt.

[6] A blast furnace reducing iron ore to iron works best with lumps of ore. Very fine material needs either agglomerating or a different process which does not require a hot gas flow through it.

[7] Due to better design and materials the mass on aluminium drink cans was reduced by over 20% from 1972 to 1988, and motor cars use about 30% less steel than similar sized predecessors of the 1960s.

[8] At present most hydrogen is made from steam reforming of natural gas, but in future it may be made on a commercial scale by electrolysis from renewable or nuclear electricity, or by nuclear-fuelled thermochemical processes.

[9] Asserting the importance of an option value of resources for some time in the future tends to ignore the dynamics of the economic process sketched here, and presupposes too much regarding future demand for particular commodities. Cobalt and tin are two metals whose use has declined sharply due to substitutes being found following scarcity and/or high prices in the last 30 years.

[10] Matt Ridley, 2001 Price Phillip lecture, RSA (www.rsa.org.uk)

[11] Based on Hubbert's methodology. Others suggest the peak will be about 2025, assuming the economic viability of unconventional resources including oil shales.

[12] See for example charts in Simon 1996 and Lomborg 2001.

[13] See Bob Raymond, 1983 *Out of the Fiery Furnace*, Macmillan, and the TV series it was part of—a project which I was intimately involved with over three years.

[14] The Mining Minerals & Sustainable Development report says that for the minerals sector, 'the goal should be to maximise the contribution to

the well-being of the current generation in a way that ensures an equitable distribution of its costs and benefits, without reducing the potential for future generations to meet their own needs.' (IIED 2002)

[15] IIED 2002, ch 5.

[16] This is in fact indicated in official figures if those covering estimates of all conventional resources are considered—9.7 million tonnes, which is 140 years' supply at today's rate of consumption. This still ignores the technological factors mentioned in the next paragraph, and unconventional resources such as phosphate deposits (22 million tonnes U) and seawater (up to 4000 Mt). From time to time concerns are raised that the known resources might be insufficient when judged as a multiple of present rate of use. But this is the Limits to Growth fallacy, a major intellectual blunder recycled from the 1970s, which takes no account of the very limited nature of the knowledge we have at any time of what is actually in the Earth's crust.

[17] Fast neutron reactors, i.e., using fast neutrons to cause fission, can be operated so as to breed more fissile material than they consume, or to incinerate fissile material such as plutonium from weapons.

[18] This is under a US$ 12 billion contract signed in 1994 for 500 tonnes of high-enriched uranium (HEU) over 20 years from 1999. In September 2005 this program reached its halfway point of 250 tonnes HEU, producing some 7500 t of low-enriched uranium fuel and with the US agent claiming the elimination of 10,000 nuclear warheads.

[19] In CANDU reactors or in reactors specially designed for this purpose. Neutron-efficient reactors, such as CANDU, are capable of operating on a thorium fuel cycle, once they are started using a fissile material such as U-235 or Pu-239. Then the thorium (Th-232) captures a neutron in the reactor to become fissile uranium (U-233), which continues the reaction.

[20] The focus here is on energy, notably electricity, but uranium used in nuclear reactors is also the basis of most nuclear medicine and a host of industrial radioisotope uses.

[21] A major problem with nuclear power, even in countries where it provides a significant portion of the electricity, is that its routine and reliable operation is little known, while any incidents receive lavish media attention.

[22] If only because plutonium was created during the operation of the Oklo natural nuclear reactors some 2000 million years ago.

[23] Both from reprocessed spent fuel, and in fast breeder reactors which are well proven (200+ reactor-years) and will become economic if and

when uranium prices rise significantly.

[24] Strictly: RTGs—radioisotope thermoelectric generators.

[25] Pu-238 is used in these applications as it has a high level of decay heat—0.56 w/g and a half life of 88 years.

[26] Instead of today's 0.7%, the fissile U-235 level was then 3-4% in the natural uranium—the level to which natural uranium needs to be enriched today, and rainwater moderated the fast neutrons, enabling the chain reaction to continue.

[27] Like plutonium, formed due to neutron capture by uranium in a fission reactor.

[28] See previous footnote. The half life of U-238 is about 4.5 billion years (the same as the age of the Earth), the half life of U-235 is shorter (700 million years), so extrapolating backwards confirms the 2 billion years since such a natural reactor could have operated.

[29] Genesis 1:1-26.

[30] 'Growth in numbers . . . requires growth in material production and provision. God provided for that need both in the astounding and incalculable riches of the legacy he put at man's disposal in the earth's crust and in the equally incalculable endowment of ingenuity and adaptability he gave to mankind himself' (Wright 1983, pp. 69-70).

[31] Ex 3:8, Dt 8:7-10.

[32] If it is argued that knowledge regarding unlocking the power of the atom is a modern manifestation of the presumption in seeking the fruit representing the knowledge of good and evil in Eden, I would disagree on two counts: first, such a position would call into question the legitimacy of all science, and second, we are following a command rather than disobeying one.

[33] The Chernobyl disaster in 1986 was a terrible tragedy which for the first time put nuclear energy into the same hazardous league as fossil fuel energy sources—the 65 deaths and enduring environmental and health effects still being less than the consequences of, say, coal use, even if projections of possible (but by no means certain or inevitable) cancer deaths are factored in. However, the fact of the Chernobyl accident makes a repetition much less likely, since there has been unprecedented international collaboration over the last decade to improve the operational safety of all Soviet-designed reactors, and to close some down. In the West, there was much less to learn from the Chernobyl accident than from the 1979 Three Mile Island one—where no-one was harmed. See also: section on safety and external costs in next chapter.

NOTES

Chapter 5: Energy Choices

[1] The question of diversity is often raised, but is really a subset of security and assurance of supply.

[2] Keith Orchison, quoting an unnamed US critic, in ESAA *Electricity Supply*, March 2002.

[3] This and the 158 MWe Nysted offshore wind farm project are the survivors of cutbacks from five such wind farms by the new Danish government early in 2002.

[4] this figure appears, for instance, in a 2001 European Wind Energy Association/Greenpeace report *Wind Force 10*.

[5] Germany, with half of Europe's installed wind capacity (14,600 MWe at the end of 2003) due to generous subsidies and tariff arrangements, is already encountering major problems in utilising the output in its grid system. When the wind blows, other generating capacity—including some base-load coal plant—must be shut down but held on standby for when it ceases to blow. Peaking capacity can fill in some of the slack during calm periods, but the wind capacity is now reaching the level (about 8% of total) so that base-load plant is affected and some is running at less than half its potential, which raises costs significantly. Consumers and taxpayers thus need to pay the inflated costs for subsidised wind generation as well as higher costs for traditional sources due to inefficiencies caused by that intermittent wind availability. Base-load power sells for about EUR 2 c/kWh, while utilities are forced to buy all wind power produced for 8.6 c/kWh whenever it happens to be available.

[6] In 2005 known economic resources of uranium (3.6 million tonnes) are enough for 50 years at current rates of use, further exploration will increase this figure—I would be surprised if it does not double by 2015.

[7] Fast breeder reactors are well proven. They breed plutonium-239 from abundant uranium-238.

[8] There are also environmental and security concerns which bear upon this reprocessing question.

[9] unless the carbon dioxide arising from steam reforming of natural gas is disregarded or sequestered, but even so there is a resource constraint.

[10] Some new types of nuclear plants such as high-temperature gas cooled reactors, operating at around 950-1000°C have the potential for producing hydrogen from water by thermochemical means, without using natural gas.

[11] The first is sometimes called the deontological (principal-based)

position, the second utilitarian.

[12] In relation to civil nuclear wastes from power generation there has never been an occasion when that containment and management has failed or caused any harm to anyone or any environmental degradation (unless one includes the Chernobyl accident which was anomalous in many respects and not relevant to waste management).

[13] This assertion is sometimes queried because it is contrary to much of the folklore. In fact virtually all nuclear wastes are contained and managed with a view to disposal. The cost of all this, including conservative allowance for future disposal, is internalised (cf., later section on external costs). So is plant decommissioning cost in most situations. Fossil fuel burning results in the release of carbon dioxide to the environment, without any internalised cost, and often many pollutants are released as well, again without internal costing.

[14] More than one third of the 25 billion tonnes per year of carbon dioxide emission from fossil fuels is due to power generation.

[15] This is not trivial, as methane—the main constituent of natural gas—is a powerful greenhouse gas.

[16] World Coal Institute, or 'Clean Coal' Technology paper on WNA web site www.world-nuclear.org. 'Burying' the CO_2 means sequestration into geological strata such as deep saline aquifers.

[17] In the EU a total of 160 000 tonnes of radioactive waste of all kinds is produced each year compared with 20 million tonnes of toxic chemical waste (which remains hazardous indefinitely).

[18] In the Introduction I also referred to the ideological aspect of the anti-nuclear campaign. It is well expressed by the prominent US energy guru and anti nuclear activist Amory Lovins: 'If nuclear power were clean, safe, economic, assured of ample fuel, and socially benign per se, it would still be unattractive because of the political implications of the kind of energy economy it would lock us into.' (Lovins, 1977, Soft Energy Paths, Ballinger) One wonders how many of the 31 countries now using it are politically unattractive because of it!

[19] In Victoria, 65 million tonnes of brown coal is burned annually for electricity. This contains about 1.6 ppm uranium and 3.0-3.5 ppm thorium, hence about 100 tonnes of uranium and 200 tonnes of thorium is buried in landfill each year in the Latrobe Valley. Australia exports 88 Mt/yr of steaming coal averaging 1.1 ppm U and 3.5 ppm Th in it, hence 100 tonnes of uranium and 300 tonnes of thorium could conceivably be added to published export figures; maybe double this if the 87 Mt/yr of exported coking

coal is similar. The actual radioactivity levels in flyash are not great. CSIRO figures give 160—200 MBq/kg for flyash in New South Wales.

[20] *Trends in the Nuclear Fuel Cycle*, OECD/NEA 2001, p 18.

[21] There is also a theory that the heat comes from a continuing fast-neutron fission reaction in the earth's core, but this has not gained wide acceptance., whereas the radiogenic heat theory is uncontroversial. See also WNA information paper on *Cosmic Origins and Geological Role of Uranium*, by Richard Arculus.

[22] Claudio Pescatore 1999, *Long-term management of radioactive waste, ethics and the environment*, NEA Newsletter # 1/99.

[23] Rio de Janiero, 1992.

[24] *Severe Accidents in the Energy Sector*, Paul Scherrer Institut, 2001.

[25] It considers over 15,000 fatalities related to oil, over 8000 related to coal and 5000 from hydro.

[26] Nuclear power delivers some 2500 TWh per year, hence these 8 deaths would be spread over 3.5 years in the course of providing 16% of the world's electricity, whereas coal's 342 deaths can be expected every 19 months for slightly more than twice the amount of electricity.

[27] In particular, 11 VVER-440/230 types and 13 RBMK types have serious design deficiencies, and one of the latter type precipitated the 1986 Chernobyl disaster.

[28] In fact Chernobyl is the only event detracting from an almost impeccable record in commercial nuclear power, and Chernobyl is of very little relevance to the actual safety of most of the world's reactors.

[29] The report itself is elusive, but details have been published by European Commission 25/7/01 and there are updates to August 2005. See <www.externe.info>.

[30] Nuclear energy averages 0.4 euro cents/kWh, much the same as hydro, coal is over 4.0 cents (4.1–7.3 cent averages in different countries), gas ranges 1.3-2.3 cents and only wind shows up better than nuclear, at 0.1-0.2 cents/kWh average.

[31] Krewitt et al., 1999, 'Environmental damage costs from fossil electricity generation in Germany and Europe', *Energy Policy* 27, 173-183.

[32] WNA 2005, Information Paper *Energy Balances and CO_2 Implications*.

[33] No reputable figures put the total higher than 8.7% of output, and some of the components of that figure are open to challenge.

[34] France is now the world's largest net exporter of electricity, 75-80% of which is nuclear-generated.

Chapter 6: Contested Ground

[1] Hore-Lacy I. & Parr-Smith G, 1995.

[2] The World Health Organisation in 1997 presented two estimates, of 2.7 or 3 million deaths occurring each year as a result of air pollution. In the latter estimate: 2.8 million deaths were due to indoor exposures and 200,000 to outdoor exposure. The lower estimate comprised 1.85 million deaths from rural indoor pollution, 363,000 from urban indoor pollution and 511,000 from urban ambient pollution. The WHO report points out that these totals are about 6% of all deaths, and the uncertainty of the estimates means that the range should be taken as 1.4 to 6 million deaths annually attributable to air pollution. WHO 1997, *Health and Environment in Sustainable Development five years after the Earth Summit.*

[3] *Against Nature* TV program, 1998.

[4] E.g., Ehrlich 1970, pp. 69-75 on non-renewable mineral resources.

[5] This version in *The Australian Financial Review* 11/6/04. He has long advocated the views quoted, but a new statement of them published in the *Independent* (UK) on 24/5/04 got wide media coverage. It concluded:

'Opposition to nuclear energy is based on irrational fear fed by Hollywood-style fiction, the Green lobbies and the media. These fears are unjustified, and nuclear energy from its start in 1952 has proved to be the safest of all energy sources. We must stop fretting over the minute statistical risks of cancer from chemicals or radiation. Nearly one third of us will die of cancer anyway, mainly because we breathe air laden with that all pervasive carcinogen, oxygen. If we fail to concentrate our minds on the real danger, which is global warming, we may die even sooner, as did more than 20,000 unfortunates from overheating in Europe last summer.

'I find it sad and ironic that the UK, which leads the world in the quality of its Earth and climate scientists, rejects their warnings and advice, and prefers to listen to the Greens. But I am a Green and I entreat my friends in the movement to drop their wrongheaded objection to nuclear energy.

'Even if they were right about its dangers, and they are not, its worldwide use as our main source of energy would pose an insignificant threat compared with the dangers of intolerable and lethal heat waves and sea levels rising to drown every coastal city of the world. We have no time to experiment with visionary energy sources; civilisation is in imminent danger and has to use nuclear—the one safe, available, energy source—now or suffer the pain soon to be inflicted by our outraged planet.'

[6] Matt Ridley, *Technology and the Environment—the case for optimism*, RSA Prince Philip lecture, May 2001.

[7] See Simon 1996.

[8] 'The environment is in poor shape here on Earth. Our resources are running out. The [ever-growing population] leaves less and less to eat. The air and water are becoming ever more polluted. The planet's species are becoming extinct in vast numbers. The forests are disappearing, fish stocks are collapsing and the coral reefs are dying. We are defiling our Earth, the fertile topsoil is disappearing, we are paving over nature, destroying the wilderness, decimating the biosphere, and will end up killing ourselves in the process. The world's ecosystem is breaking down. We are fast approaching the absolute limit of viability, and the limits of growth are becoming apparent'—as represented in chapter 1.

[9] *Economist* leader 2/2/02.

[10] Lomborg does not identify with the climate change sceptics who say that the scientific evidence is insufficient to indicate a major problem. Some well-qualified scientists do take this position.

[11] www.lomborg.com

[12] www.greenspirit.com/lomborg

[13] These are very similar to earlier opposition to Julian Simon by *Science* journal and others, see Simon 1996, epilogue.

[14] This is also a weakness, UN agencies can only report what member government tell them, and some data sets relying at some point on subjective judgement are therefore suspect, and have been treated so in chapter 2.

[15] Lomborg 2001, p 352.

[16] John 8:32.

[17] Both in *Against Nature* TV series.

[18] In *Against Nature* TV series.

[19] Several authors highlight the Romantic roots of environmentalism. Possibly the most informative is Veldman 1994—see appendix.

[20] Simon 1996.

Select Bibliography

Alexander, Denis. *Rebuilding the Matrix: Science and Faith in the 21st Century* (Oxford: Lio n, 2001).

Barns, Ian. 'Two Views on Managing the Earth's Resources', Zadok paper S82, 1996, Melbourne, Australia.

Beisner, E. Calvin. *Prospects for Growth: A Biblical View Population, Resources and the Future* (Wheaton, Ill.: Crossway Books, 1990).

Berry, R.J. *God and the Biologist: Faith at the Frontiers of Science* Apollos (Leicester: Apollos, 1996).

Berry, R.J. (ed) *The Care of Creation: Focusing Concern and Action* (Leicester: Inter-Varsity Press, 2000).

Berry, R.J. *God's Book of Works: The Nature and Theology of Nature* (London: T&T Clark, 2003).

Birch, C., et al. *Liberating Life: Contemporary Approaches to Ecological Theory* (Maryknoll, N.Y.: Orbis Books, 1990)

Bouma-Prediger, S. *For the Beauty of the Earth: A Christian Vision for Creation Care* (Grand Rapids: Baker Academic, 2001).

Bradley, Ian. *God is Green: Ecology for Christians* (London: Darton Longman & Todd, 1990).

Brown, Cavan. *Pilgrim Through this Barren Land* (Sydney: Albatross Books, 1991).

Bruce, Donald & Horrocks, Don (eds) *Modifying Creation? GM Crops and Foods: A Christian Perspective.* An Evangelical Alliance Policy Commission Report (Carlisle: Paternoster, 2001).

Chase, Alston. *In a Dark Wood: The Fight over Forests and the Rising Tyranny of Ecology* (New York: Houghton Mifflin Co, 1995).

Clark, Stephen R.L. *How to Think about the Earth: Philosophical and Theological Models for Ecology* (London: Mowbray, 1993).

Clarke, Jonathan. 'Is the Past the Key to the Future? Forty Years of Young Earth Creationism', *Pacific J. Sci & Theol* (2001) 2,1.

Clatworthy, Jonathan. *Good God: Green Theology and the Value of Creation* (Charlbury: John Carpenter, 1997).

Cobb, John. *Is It Too Late? A Theology of Ecology* (Beverly Hills, Calif.: Environmental Ethics Books, 1972).

Cohen, Maurie J. *'Evidence of a New Environmentalism: Investor and Consumer Activism as Expressions of Postmaterial Values'.* OCEES Research paper # 10 (Oxford, 1997).

Collins, Paul, 1995, *God's Earth: Religion as if Matter Really Mattered* (North Blackburn, Vic.: Dove, 1995).

Cromartie, Michael(ed). *Creation at Risk? Religion, Science and Environmentalism* (Grand Rapids: Eerdmans-Ethics & Public Policy Center, 1995).

Deane-Drummond, Celia. *A Handbook of Theology and Ecology* (London: SCM Press, 1996).

Derr, Thomas (with James Nash & Richard John Neuhaus). *Environmental Ethics and Christian Humanism* (Nashville, Tenn.: Abingdon Press, 1996).

De-Shalit, Avner. *Where Philosophy Meets Politics: The Concept of Environment*, OCEES Research paper # 13 (Oxford, 1997).

De Soto, Hernando. *The Mystery of Capital: Why Capitalism Triumphs in the West and Fails Everywhere Else* (New York: Basic Books, 2000).

De Witt, Calvin (ed) *The Environment and the Christian: What Does the New Testament Say about the Environment?* (Grand Rapids: Baker, 1991).

Ehrlich, Paul & Ann. *Population, Resources Environment: Issues in Human Ecology* (San Francisco: W. H. Freeman, 1970).

Gnanakan, Ken. *God's World: A Theology of the Environment* (London: SPCK, 1999).

Granberg-Michaelson, Wesley. *Redeeming the Creation: The Earth Summit: Challenges for Christians* (Geneva: WCC, 1992).

Gray, John. *Straw Dogs* (London: Granta Books, 2002).

Gregg, Samuel. *Beyond Romanticism: Questioning the Green Gospel* (Sydney, Australia: Centre for Independent Studies, 2000).

Hall, Douglas John. *Imaging God: Dominion as Stewardship* (Grand Rapids: Eerdmans, 1986).

Hall, Douglas John. *The Steward: A Biblical Symbol Come of Age* (Grand Rapids: Eerdmans, 1990).

Hargrove, Eugene C. *Foundations of Environmental Ethics* (Englewood Cliffs, N.J.: Prentice Hall, 1989).

Hodgson, Peter E. *Nuclear Power: Energy and the Environment* (London: Imperial College Press, 1999).

Hore-Lacy, I. & Parr-Smith. G. *Enhancing Nature Conservation through Complementary Land Use* (Minerals Council of Australia, 1995),

Hore-Lacy, I. *Creating Common Wealth: Aspects of Public Theology in Economics* (Oxford: Lion, 1985).

Houghton, Sir John. *Christian Challenge of Caring for the Earth*, John Ray Initiative <www.jri.org.uk/ brief/christianchallenge.htm>.

Houghton, Sir John. *Global Warming: The Complete Briefing*, 3rd ed. (Cambridge University Press, 2004).

International Institute for Environment & Development, *Breaking New Ground: Mining, Minerals & Sustainable Development* (2002) MMSD final report <www.iied.org/mmsd/finalreport/copies.html>.

Irwin, Kevin W & Pellegrino, Edmond D (eds). *Preserving the Creation: Environmental Theology and Ethics* (Washington: Georgetown University Press, 1994).

Jeeves, Malcolm A. & Berry, R.J. *Science, Life and Christian Belief: A Survey and Assessment* (Leicester: Apollos, 1998).

John Paul II. *Sollicitudo Rei Socialis: On Social Concerns* (London: St. Paul Publications, 1988).

Josephson, Paul R. *Red Atom: Russia's Nuclear Power Program from Stalin to Today* (New York: W. H. Freeman & Co., 1999).

Landes, David S. *The Unbound Prometheus: Technological Change and Industrial Development in Western Europe from 1750 to the Present.* 2nd ed. (Cambridge University Press, 2003).

Lilburne, Geoff. *A Sense of Place: A Christian theology of the Land* (Nashville, Tenn.: Abingdon Press, 1989).

Lomborg, Bjorn *The Skeptical Environmentalist: Measuring the Real State of the World* (Cambridge University Press, 2001).

Lovelock, James. *Gaia: A New Look at Life on Earth* (Oxford University Press, 1979).

Lovelock, James. *The Ages of Gaia* (Oxford University Press, 1988).

McDonagh, Sean, *To Care for the Earth: A Call to a New Theology* (London: Geoffrey Chapman, 1986).

McFague, Sallie. 'Imaging a Theology of Nature: the world as God's body', in Birch (ed) op cit.

McGrath, Alister. *The Re-enchantment of Nature: Science, Religion and the Human Sense of Wonder* (London: Hodder & Stoughton, 2003).

McNeill, John Robert. *Something New Under the Sun: An Environmental History of the Twentieth Century* (London: Penguin Books, 2001).

Meadows, D. et al. *The Limits to Growth* (New York: Universe Books, 1972).

Moltmann, Jürgen. *God in Creation: An Ecological Doctrine of Creation* (London: SCM Press, 1985).

Nash, James A. *Loving Nature: Ecological Integrity and Christian Responsibility* (Nashville, Tenn.: Abingdon Press with Churches' Center for Theology and Public Policy, 1991).

Nash, Roderick F. *The Rights of Nature: A History of Environmental Ethics* (University of Wisconsin Press 1989; Primavera Press, 1990).

Northcott, Michael S. *The Environment and Christian Ethics* (Cambridge University Press, 1996).

O'Donovan, Oliver. *Resurrection and Moral Order: An Outline for Evangelical Ethics.* 2nd ed. (Leicester: Apollos, 1986).

Osborn, Lawrence. *Guardians of Creation: Nature in Theology and the Christian life* (Leicester: Apollos, 1993).

Page, Ruth. *God and the Web of Creation* (London: SCM Press, 1996).

Passmore, John. *Man's Responsibility for Nature* (London: Duckworth, 1974).

Peacocke, A. R. *Creation and the World of Science* (Oxford: Clarendon Press, 1979).

Pescatore, Claudio. 'Long-term Management of Radioactive Waste, Ethics and the Environment', *NEA Newsletter*, No. 1/99, OECD Paris.

Plimer, Ian. *Telling Lies for God: Reason versus Creationism* (Milsons Point, NSW: Random House Australia, 1994).

Ridley, Matt. 'Technology and the Environment: the case for optimism', RSA Prince Philip lecture, May 2001 <www.rsa.org.uk>.

Royal Society. *Genetically Modified Plants for Food Use* (London: The Royal Society, 1998)

Royal Society. *Non-Food Crops* (London: The Royal Society, 1999).

Royal Society. *Transgenic Plants and World Agriculture* (London: The Royal Society, 2000)

Royal Society. *Genetically Modified Plants for Food Use & Human Consumption: An Update* (London: The Royal Society, 2002).

Schaeffer, Francis A. *Pollution and the Death of Man* (Tyndale House, 1970).

Seaton, Chris. *Whose Earth?* (Cambridge: Crossway Books, 1992).

Sheehan, James. *Global Greens: Inside the International Environmental Establishment* (Washington: Capital Research Center, 1998).

Simon, Julian L. *The Ultimate Resource 2* (Princeton, N.J.: Princeton University Press, 1996).

Smil, Vaclav. *Enriching the Earth: Fritz Haber, Carl Bosch, and the transformation of world food production* (Cambridge, Mass.: MIT Press, 2000).

Stott, John R. W. *New Issues facing Christians Today* (London: Marshall Pickering, 1999).

Tacey, David. 'Prospects for Re-enchantment', *Zadok Perspectives* (Melbourne, Australia: 2000) 67.

Tolkien, J. R. R. *The Lord of the Rings* (London: George Allen & Unwin, 1969).

Veldman, M. *Fantasy, the Bomb, and the Greening of Britain: Romantic Protest 1945-1980* (Cambridge University Press, 1994).

Walter, J. A. *The Human Home: The Myth of the Sacred Environment* (Oxford: Lion, 1982).

Weart, Spencer 1988, *Nuclear Fear: A History of Images,* Harvard University Press, USA.

White, Lynn 1967, 'The Historical Roots of our Ecological Crisis', *Science,* vol. 155, pp. 1203-07 (reprinted in Schaeffer, *Pollution and the Death of Man,* 1970).

Wilkinson, Loren, *Earthkeeping in the Nineties: Stewardship of Creation.* Rev. ed. (Grand Rapids: Eerdmans, 1991).

World Commission on Environment and Development. *Our Common Future* (Brundtland Report, 1987).

World Nuclear Association, 2004, Information Papers: 'Energy Analysis of Power Systems, Sustainable Energy, Thorium' <www.worldnuclear.org> London, UK.

Wright, Christopher J.H. *Living as the People of God* (Leicester: Inter-Varsity Press, 1983).

Printed in the United Kingdom
by Lightning Source UK Ltd.
108245UKS00002B/352-357